RADICAL DISCIPLESHIP

RADICAL DISCIPLESHIP
Uncompromising Conviction in a Hostile World

Hensworth W. C. Jonas

Reformation Heritage Books
Grand Rapids, Michigan

Radical Discipleship
© 2024 by Hensworth W. C. Jonas

All rights reserved. No part of this book may be used or reproduced in any manner whatsoever without written permission except in the case of brief quotations embodied in critical articles and reviews. Direct your requests to the publisher at the following addresses:

Reformation Heritage Books
3070 29th St. SE
Grand Rapids, MI 49512
616–977–0889
orders@heritagebooks.org
www.heritagebooks.org

Scripture taken from the King James Version. In the public domain.

Printed in the United States of America
24 25 26 27 28 29/10 9 8 7 6 5 4 3 2 1

Library of Congress Cataloging-in-Publication Data

Names: Jonas, Hensworth W. C., author.
Title: Radical discipleship : uncompromising conviction in a hostile world / Hensworth W.C. Jonas.
Description: Grand Rapids, Michigan : Reformation Heritage Books, [2024] | Includes bibliographical references.
Identifiers: LCCN 2023054422 (print) | LCCN 2023054423 (ebook) | ISBN 9798886860948 (paperback) | ISBN 9798886860955 (epub)
Subjects: LCSH: Commitment (Psychology)—Religious aspects—Christianity. | Commitment (Psychology) | Christian life.
Classification: LCC BV4597.53.C56 J56 2024 (print) | LCC BV4597.53.C56 (ebook) | DDC 248.4—dc23/eng/20240129
LC record available at https://lccn.loc.gov/2023054422
LC ebook record available at https://lccn.loc.gov/2023054423

For additional Reformed literature, request a free book list from Reformation Heritage Books at the above regular or email address.

DEDICATION

For to me to live is Christ, and to die is gain.
—PHILIPPIANS 1:21

I DEDICATE THIS SMALL VOLUME TO
the wife of my youth,
Vandah M. Jonas,
and, in the happy providence of God,
to the family He has given us:

Our son—
the Rev. Joshua M. Jonas, and his wife, Chanda G. Jonas

Our daughter—
Stephanie H. Lewis, and her husband,
the Rev. Rolando A. Lewis

Our daughter—
Nia A. S. Jonas

Our two grandchildren—
Charity Jennifer Elizabeth Jonas and
Elias William Benjamin Jonas

Lo, children are an heritage of the LORD:
and the fruit of the womb is his reward.
—PSALM 127:3

CONTENTS

Introduction ix
1. Radical Christ 1
2. Radical Transformation 15
3. Radical Worship 27
4. Radical Prayer 37
5. Radical Suffering 49
6. Radical Resistance 61
7. Radical Missions 71
8. Radical Marriage 81
9. Radical Labor 91
10. Radical Perspective 101
Conclusion 109

INTRODUCTION

By the time this small volume is printed, I will have completed thirty-seven years of pastoral ministry in the Central Baptist Church of Radio Range, St. John's, Antigua and Barbuda. My twin-island nation is an independent member state of the British Commonwealth in the eastern Caribbean. It is considered a developing nation even though life on these islands, in many respects, resembles the style found in the major powers of the West.

My ministry involved the founding of the East Caribbean Baptist Mission, our indigenous mission agency, through which I led a local television broadcast for over three decades, church planting initiatives, Christian education (early childhood, primary, and secondary), and international itinerant preaching. In 2011, my nation officially honored me for my work in education administration with the Grand Cross of the Most Distinguished Order of Princely Heritage (GCH). I have fought the culture wars on issues like abortion and homosexuality on local talk radio and through lobbying efforts with the political directorate.

I believe that this background has positioned me to make an informed evaluation of the state of Christianity in my country, our Caribbean civilization, and the larger Western world. I am convinced that an effeminate, cowardly, perverted, and shallow iteration of Christianity has the ascendancy in our generation.

Many church members are nominal Christians, ignorant of the faith's biblical foundations, the history of the church, and the content of classical Christian theology. They are not confessionally grounded and have given only formal assent to the church's historic creeds and catechisms. Practically, neither the Holy Scriptures nor these documents inform their personal decisions, vocational commitments, moral convictions, and worldview. If they are not officially atheists, they are not far from it.

The problem is that they still insist they are Christians. This creates confusion in both polemics and apologetics, and it is a nightmare both pastorally and evangelistically. The sharp contrast between the Christian lifestyle and worldliness has been blurred in the broader culture, or even eliminated in particular contexts. The culture seems to be driving contemporary Christian ethics and morality, even while the church, in general, still maintains that its biblical mandate and agenda is to impact the culture for Christ. Why should the world convert to a religious version of what it already professes?

The most popular brands of Christianity today generally make no severe demands on their followers. It is believed that the last thing this generation will accept is more structure. The mood of the times is that the "self" and its tenacious pursuit of acceptance and comfort must be pampered at all costs. A radical narcissism is encouraged. Many churches are now determined to give the masses emotional ecstasy, theatrical excitement, sensual music, and absolution without biblical repentance. Of course, all this comes with the clever manipulation and abuse of particular biblical texts to give this capitulation some semblance of legitimacy. The last thing such gullible people want is a biblical church that expects them to conscientiously affirm the lordship of Christ, to know and live by the historic creeds, and to obey the commandments of Christ. Church discipline is seriously challenged because religious competition between denominations—and even within denominations—allows an errant adherent under discipline by one church to find a religious group around the corner that will legitimize all their lusts. These groups, whether by intentional policy affirmations or inadvertently through a culture of laxity, remain silent while their followers pursue iniquity with a passion.

True churches cannot allow this, even if it means a loss of members. Genuine Bible-believing churches (not just those who say they are Bible-believing or have "Bible" in their name) will refuse to accommodate the sensual demands of our times. They will declare the doctrine of the holiness of God and make abundantly clear the demands of that holiness upon every life. The general downgrade in our churches is directly linked to ignorance of, or contempt for, the holiness of God.

When Scripture calls God "holy" (Lev. 11:44), the word means that God is in a category all by Himself. This revelation makes God an object of adoration, dread, and awe. The holiness of God is an element of all His attributes, whether communicable or incommunicable, for it covers all aspects of His moral perfection and transcendent majesty. God's holiness primarily has to do with His purity. The God of the Bible has zero tolerance for sin. It is written in Habakkuk 1:13, "Thou art of purer eyes than to behold evil, and canst not look on iniquity." Every sinner is commanded to abase themselves in God's holy presence. This is what happened to the prophet Isaiah in his vision of the presence of the Lord. The prophet cried out, "Woe is me! for I am undone; because I am a man of unclean lips, and I dwell in the midst of a people of unclean lips: for mine eyes have seen the King, the LORD of hosts" (Isa. 6:5).

God's moral law, requiring conduct that matches His own, is "holy, and just, and good" (Rom. 7:12). He always judges justly, according to what we deserve. God's active hostility to sin, His wrath, is impeccably just in all its manifestations, and His particular retributive punishments are so glorious that they invoke doxology of the highest order. What is more, God's justice is not compromised when He acts to save His people. The fulfillment of His covenant commitment to rescue the elect of every nation is utterly consistent with His justice. He punishes our sins in the person of Christ, our substitute. The form taken by His justifying mercy in Christ shows Him to be perfectly and consistently just (Rom. 3:26).

The radical departure of our generation from the truth in favor of an anemic Christianity must be answered with a radical return to orthodoxy and orthopraxy. The God of the Bible affirms His holy purity by revealing that He is light, with no darkness in Him at all

(1 John 1:5). Every regenerate and forgiven believer is summoned to practice a holiness that will testify to their identification with God's holiness, even though their holiness is imperfectly expressed. Because God is holy, God's people must also be holy (Lev. 11:44).

In the New Testament, the apostle Peter quotes this passage from Leviticus, giving us a clear picture of the rationale for a return to a more radicalized Christianity (see 1 Peter 1:13–16). He points out that we must be radical for Christ in separating ourselves from this world and imitating God, knowing that our time here on earth is short and this world is not our home.

Anticipating the Future

Peter writes, "Wherefore gird up the loins of your mind, be sober, and hope to the end for the grace that is to be brought unto you at the revelation of Jesus Christ" (1 Peter 1:13). The central thought in this verse is expressed in the command "hope to the end." The essence and heart of this command is to persist in living out who we are. We are to realize in our actual experience what God has accomplished on our behalf by His grace. The verse gives a strong note of urgency to the command, implying the purposeful adoption of a new attitude of mind and heart. We are called to wait for the Lord in joyful anticipation of the completion of the good work He has begun within us (Phil. 1:6). This hope is strong, wholehearted, and unwavering in its expectancy and desire.

We are also called to make an intellectual effort that demands preparation, sobriety, and discipline. Because of the long flowing robes that men wore in those times, it was necessary for them, before engaging in strenuous physical activity, to gather up their robes and tuck them under their belts at the waist. Today, we would probably say, "Roll up your sleeves" or "Pull yourself together." Christian hope requires the use of vigorous concentration and determined resolution as we focus our attention on the Lord's return.

The last thing of interest for many in this generation—and yet the very thing that is urgently needed—is the desire for strenuous thinking. Contemporary churchgoers have a pathetic expectation of brevity and levity in the pulpit. There is often a painful numerical attrition in the membership of the churches that refuse to acquiesce to this desire and to pander to popular tastes. Biblical churches, however, must resist this vagabond laziness that is determined to dumb down the intellectual and spiritual discourse of the local church. They must be committed to fighting the ignorance of those with no genuine interest in spiritual things by engaging in profound interaction with biblical truth, such as the attributes of God and the sufficiency of Christ's atoning sacrifice on Calvary. The faithful will not let anything distract us from prosecuting, with great discipline, the spiritual warfare around us.

Sobriety is a favorite theme with the apostle Peter (1 Peter 1:13). We may associate the idea with the avoidance of drunkenness, and it certainly includes that. But it evolved in the context of the church to refer to a self-control and clarity of mind that leads to wisdom in conduct, speech, and judgment. Since our time on earth is short and our task is serious, there is no room for reckless fanaticism or self-indulgence. There must be a determined focus on the goal of our journey that looks up continually to our heavenly Zion, while still looking forward to avoid stumbling.

The focus of our gaze must always be upward and forward, not backward or around us. There must be a longing in our hearts for the beautiful city of God, combined with a holy indifference to the things of this world that we will all inevitably leave behind us. Even the good things in our lives should not be allowed to own us. There must be a readiness in the twinkling of an eye to trade this mortality for immortality, and the corruptible for that which is incorruptible (1 Cor. 15:51–52). Our commitment must be to that "continuing city" (Heb. 13:14) whose builder and maker is God (Heb. 11:8–10).

Separation from the Worldliness

Peter goes on, "As obedient children, not fashioning yourselves according to the former lusts in your ignorance" (1 Peter 1:14). Peter's gentile hearers were to mortify the evil desires that characterized their past pagan lives. It is a totalitarian call to turn one's life in a new direction, ceasing to conform to the manners and morals of pagan society. Peter's readers were to be motivated and incentivized by the new paradigm in which they now lived, as obedient children of God. They rejected the pretentious autonomy that is the essence of rebellion against the true and living God. In its place was a call to integrity—to be known consistently for their obedience to God.

True believers in Jesus Christ have no interest in blending in with the status quo. Because obedience to Christ is our new identity, we will, of necessity, become subversives who are determined to undermine the wicked and perverse world in which we must now live. Thus, we will refuse to cooperate with any academic curriculum that pretends the human mind is ultimate. We will not accept any ideology that declares that matter creates itself. We will not support any political agenda that legitimizes what God calls an abomination. We will not tolerate any attempt to diminish the value of human life. We will not become anarchists who reject the use of legitimate authority. We will not join any effort to undermine or prejudice the truth of God. We will not encourage the temptation to foster discontentment, greed, and covetousness. We are biblical separatists and radicals, and we will never accept the corruption of this world, no matter how strongly it infiltrates the environment around us.

Imitating Our God

Peter concludes this section of his epistle by saying, "But as he which hath called you is holy, so be ye holy in all manner of conversation; because it is written, Be ye holy; for I am holy" (1 Peter 1:15–16). Our radical response to the perversion of our generation is motivated by the positive command of God to be holy. The word *holy* denotes separateness, dedication, and consecration, and it is used for persons and things that have been withdrawn from ordinary use. The opposite of holy is *profane* or *common*. The word *holy* does not in itself have a particular ethical or moral connotation. Such a connotation comes from contextual considerations: the nature of that to which one is dedicated. One can be holy or separated unto either iniquity or moral purity. The apostle Peter admonishes the believers to be dedicated to the God of the Bible, a God of absolute moral purity. They, like their God, are to be marked by moral purity in a way that makes them quite distinct from people around them.

God has not only commanded but has modeled this moral purity. Verse 15 begins, "But as he which hath called you is holy," therefore God is the standard for Christian holiness. We are only to do what is consistent with God's character. When believers sin, they forget who they are. We must remember that we are not our own, for we have been bought with a price (1 Cor. 6:19–20). We are a royal priesthood, a peculiar people, God's special possession (1 Peter 2:9). We must also remember that we are dead to sin, and our life is hidden with Christ in God (Col. 3:3). We must not forget that we are joint heirs with Christ and that our inheritance is secure in Him. Thus, we cannot allow ourselves to become common and profane.

It is important to understand that this does not mean that we are proud or part of a pretentious spiritual aristocracy. We are not looking down on anyone, but we are looking up at the Lord Jesus and so we cannot be ordinary, for our Savior is extraordinary—He is altogether lovely. We cannot engage in the works of darkness, for our God is light, and in Him there is no darkness at all. We cannot be profane, for we have an exalted calling to share in Christ's ministry of reconciliation. Our life must be consistent with our eternal destination. We will dwell forever in the very presence of the immortal, invisible, only wise God. As the Scottish pastor John Brown once wrote, "Holiness does not consist in mystic speculations, enthusiastic fervours, or uncommanded austerities; it consists in thinking as God thinks and willing as God wills."[1]

---

1. John Brown, *Expository Discourses on the First Epistle of the Apostle Peter* (1866; repr., Edinburgh: Banner of Truth, 1980), 1.106.

Chapter 1

RADICAL CHRIST

Every generation has a romantic fascination with the revolutionary personality—the radical. We gravitate toward people with the charisma, eloquence, courage, and vision to challenge the status quo and change the trajectory of their world. These people are memorialized in city monuments. At first sight, the call of Matthew, one of the original followers of Jesus Christ, may not seem very radical. Matthew 9:9 tells us, "And as Jesus passed forth from thence, he saw a man, named Matthew, sitting at the receipt of custom: and he saith unto him, Follow me. And he arose, and followed him." But a closer look at this call reveals a radicalism typical of authentic Christian discipleship. We see it clearly when our focus rests not on Matthew but on the Christ who called him. Christ is indeed a radical who revolutionizes the lives of His followers.

In this book, we will consider the motivations and characteristics of a true Christ-follower who has been radicalized, in contrast to those who remain passive and indifferent. Of course, by "radicals" we do *not* refer to anything resembling the disciples of the death cult of Islam. We refer to the life-transforming boldness, focus, discipline, and outlook of one who is a genuine recipient of the love of Jesus Christ. We speak of radical Christian love and the expected effects of that posture toward the world around us.

It is obvious that many who profess belief in Christianity do not live radical lives for Christ. Rather, they are bogged down with insignificant matters and immobilized by trivial relational squabbles. Why are they not radical for Christ, like the heroes of the faith listed in Hebrews 11, who lived exemplary lives of greatness in service of their Savior? It seems that many who claim faith in Christ do not truly understand Christianity. On the contrary, they are deluded about the essence of the faith and Christian living.

Biblical Christianity is an unparalleled movement in history—there is nothing in human experience that resembles it. Many people imagine that Christianity is essentially just like other religions, but Matthew's call makes it clear that the message the Lord Jesus Christ brings to us is unique and unprecedented—absolutely new! Everyone who becomes a faithful, biblical Christian has had a sense of being rudely awakened from their slumber. We may have thought that we understood Christ and Christianity at one point, but then, all of a sudden, a light came on for us. We heard ourselves saying, whether out loud or in our inmost thoughts, "This faith is radically different!" That was certainly Matthew's experience.

The disparity in radicalization among professing Christ-followers can be explained by examining their understanding of the faith. Not everyone understands Christ's message, nor are all professions of faith equally valid. In Paul's epistle to the Colossians, he wrote about the gospel,

> Which is come unto you, as it is in all the world; and bringeth forth fruit, as it doth also in you, since the day ye heard of it, and knew the grace of God in truth.... For this cause we also, since the day we heard it, do not cease to pray for you, and to desire that ye might be filled with the knowledge of his will in all wisdom and spiritual understanding; That ye might walk worthy of the Lord unto all pleasing, being fruitful in every good work, and increasing in the knowledge of God. (Col. 1:6, 9–10)

The early church at Colossae had encountered false teachers who claimed to provide people with unique insights and revelations. The apostle Paul countered this false teaching by drawing attention to the true source of our understanding: Christ and the gospel. He asserted that the gospel began to bear fruit in the Colossians on the day they first understood the grace of God in all its truth. He did not say that the decisive moment was the day on which they signed a decision card, filled out a form, or came down the aisle of a chapel. He did not even say it was the day when they got baptized, for baptism by itself does not make anyone a biblical Christian. Something radical had to happen on the inside for them to become children of God. Perhaps it is time for us to stop asking people about decisions they have made and religious ceremonies they have undergone and instead focus on a person's inner experience of regenerating change. Christianity is not first and foremost about the pursuit of personal happiness but rather about the pursuit of practical holiness.

The Lord Jesus made the same point in the parable of the sower in Matthew 13. In that famous parable, our Lord told the story about a sower who went out and scattered seeds onto his field. Some of the seeds fell onto each of four different kinds of ground. On one type of ground, "the way side," there was no growth at all (Matt. 13:4); on two other kinds of ground, there was only temporary growth ("upon stony places," and "among thorns" vv. 5–7); meanwhile, there was permanent, abundant growth on the last kind of soil ("good ground" v. 8).

Our Lord Jesus explained the parable like this: the seed is the Word of God, the true message of Christianity, while the four soils are four different responses to this message. On the first kind of ground (the way side), the reason nothing grows is that the Word of God is rejected. On the second and third kinds of ground (upon stony places and among thorns), there is initial growth that does not last. That is because these people receive the Word of God without serious thought and consideration. Regarding the fourth kind of ground, however, Jesus said this, "But he that received seed into the good ground is he that heareth the word, and understandeth it; which also beareth fruit, and bringeth forth, some an hundredfold, some sixty, some thirty" (Matt. 13:23).

That is a pretty radical outcome for the sower's efforts. In effect, our Lord says that if we do not see this kind of tremendous growth in our lives, it may not merely be because we have failed to apply the gospel consistently or adequately. The problem may be that we never understood it at all. The call of Matthew mentioned earlier shows us a man who certainly got it. Jesus's message was a total rejection of the religious status quo, the self-righteous spiritual authorities of His day, and all their conventions. It is a revolutionary call directed to those who recognize themselves to be wicked sinners. It will never be welcomed by the "good" people of this world, the self-righteous, who are often the most respected citizens in society.

Our Lord shows us what a genuine Christian is in this passage—they are someone who has been called by God. They did not merely decide one day to become a disciple of Christ—they were drafted into the service of Jesus, having been suddenly and miraculously made new. It is as simple as that. We are not real Christians unless we, like Matthew, have experienced a call. Christianity is not something that we embrace—it is something that embraces us. Indeed, the reason why some people put Christianity down and abandon it is simply that they took it up in their own strength. But when Christianity takes you up, it will not let you go. This is one of the main ways in which we can tell whether our faith is authentic: we will have a sense of being worked upon by an external power. We did not search for this; rather, this God came searching for us, and called us, as He did Matthew, saying, "Follow me."

This description of Christianity demands further explanation. To begin with, we have to be careful not to assume that God always works in precisely the same way in everyone's life. It is fascinating to notice the narrative that precedes the call of Matthew in Matthew 9:1–8:

> And he entered into a ship, and passed over, and came into his own city. And, behold, they brought to him a man sick of the palsy, lying on a bed: and Jesus seeing their faith said unto the sick of the palsy; Son, be of good cheer; thy sins be forgiven thee. And, behold, certain of the scribes said within themselves, This man blasphemeth. And Jesus knowing their thoughts said, Wherefore think ye evil in your hearts? For whether is easier, to say, Thy sins be forgiven thee; or to say, Arise, and walk? But that ye may know that the Son of man hath power on earth to forgive sins, (then saith he to the sick of the palsy,) Arise, take up thy bed, and go unto thine house. And he arose, and departed to

his house. But when the multitudes saw it, they marvelled, and glorified God, which had given such power unto men.

We must pay close attention to what is happening in this narrative. On the surface, our Lord Jesus's dealings with the paralytic and His dealings with Matthew are significantly different. The paralyzed man had several friends, and we are told in Mark's account that they were trying to get into the house where Jesus was speaking, but there were so many people around the house that they could not get in (Mark 2:2–3). So, they went up on the roof and tore a hole through which they could lower their friend (v. 4). We are left to wonder what the house owner must have thought of their behavior! It is clear, however, that the paralytic and his friends were in hot pursuit of our Lord Jesus.

Now contrast that account with Matthew's case. Matthew was not looking for Jesus. He was at work, seated at his desk, where he was a customs officer collecting and recording the taxes required by a foreign occupying power. Suddenly, our Lord Jesus appeared and said, "Follow me." Matthew did not expect this. He was not looking or praying for this. The Lord Jesus came up to him and issued him an order, "Follow me."

Our Lord has different ways of dealing with people. Some of us come to Christ in a crisis, while others come in a time of calm reflection. Some come after careful study and investigation, while others come to Christ in a sudden emotional experience. Some people believe it is essential to respond in a church meeting by walking to the front, while others see the proper public profession of faith as believer's baptism. There are variations in each person's experience of Jesus. However, there are at the same time some fundamental commonalities—commonalities that come from the radical power, the radical person, and the radical promise of the Lord Jesus Christ.

The Radical Power of Christ

When we first meet Matthew, he was in the crosshairs of Christ's attention. The Lord Jesus "saw a man, named Matthew, sitting at the receipt of custom" (Matt. 9:9). Like every true believer in Christ, Matthew sensed a power focusing upon him and invading his personal space. It was a power coming into his life from outside, taking charge of his life. When we are saved, most of us are not on an expedition of discovery. Instead, we are subjected to an invasion. We are not the hunters, seekers of truth; rather, we are being hunted. In our conversion, we are not in control; rather, the Lord Jesus takes charge through the Holy Spirit. This is why we speak of being called—an external power is summoning us.

This is quite obvious in Matthew's case. Matthew was minding his own business when his duties were suddenly interrupted. Yet the same was true in the case of the person with paralysis. He was not in pursuit of the person he found. He was actually looking for a different kind of Jesus—a miracle worker to heal his body from disease, not a Savior to heal his soul from sin. He was sick and his friends had heard of Jesus, the healer. He thought that Jesus was merely going to heal him. When he was lowered down with the help of his friends and Jesus said, "Your sins are forgiven," he must have thought, "What? That is not what I came here for." But Jesus was in charge; the Lord had His own agenda. The person with paralysis may have thought that he was in control of his own life, but he was utterly wrong. A *coup d'état* was in motion. He was being summoned into the service of a new master.

No sinner ever truly seeks God (see Rom. 3:11, quoting Ps. 14:1–3). We may search for a god that we have personally designed, a figment of our idolatrous imagination who will solve all our problems and heal our brokenness, but we are not looking for the God of the Bible. As soon as we learn of the attributes and identity of the true and living God, we sense that our former search was a complete farce. We were after a false god, but the real God was after us all along.

To be called is to experience an alien power at work in our lives. If we do not have that sensation that somebody is after us, then it is likely that we are not experiencing authentic Christianity. If we are not genuinely called by God, we will continue playing little games with religion or eventually come to hold Christianity in contempt.

This is why the apostle Paul wrote in 1 Corinthians 1:18, "For the preaching of the cross is to them that perish foolishness; but unto us which are saved it is the power of God." When we experience the power of such a call, we know that we will never be the same again. We have been arrested by the Holy Spirit, and far from resisting that arrest, we thank the One who executed the warrant. We waive our right to be silent, for we must now shout it from the rooftops. We affirm with boldness that we already have an attorney, an Advocate with the Father, Jesus Christ the righteous. In His custody, the bonds of Christ prove to be delightful slavery. Our incarceration paradoxically brings us an inexpressible joy that is full of glory.

Thomas Watson wrote, "Jesus Christ redeems captives, He ransoms sinners by price, and rescues them by force as David took a lamb out of the mouth of the roaring lion. Oh, what a mercy it is to be brought out of the house of bondage to be made subjects of the Prince of Peace."[1]

The Radical Person of Christ

Matthew quickly sensed, just like all who experience saving faith in Christ, that he was being confronted with a person, not just a philosophical idea or an ethical code. The Lord Jesus walked into his life and said, "Follow Me." He did not say, "Follow that." The historical Jesus Christ confronts us with His purpose and His person. This was not a narcissistic self-focus but a holy self-centeredness. If the answer to man's sinful choices and sinister inheritance is divine atonement, then the focus must necessarily be upon the sacrificial Lamb, the person of Christ. He lovingly and consistently calls attention to the only answer to man's sinful condition: His holy person. Authentic Christianity is thus always centered on the radical person of Christ. The Puritan Samuel Rutherford understood this when he wrote on January 1, 1637, "I want nothing but a further revelation of the beauty of the unknown Son of God."[2]

---

1. Thomas Watson, *The Ten Commandments* (1692; repr., Edinburgh: Banner of Truth, 1965), 41.
2. Samuel Rutherford, "Letter 75: To John Kennedy, Baillie of Ayr," *Letters of the*

Just listen to Christ. Hear His questions in Matthew 16 to His disciples. "Whom do men say that I the Son of man am?... But whom say ye that I am?" (vv. 13, 15). Here is holy self-centeredness. Or consider the narrative in Acts 9 of our Lord's encounter with the terrorist called Saul of Tarsus. Saul had been persecuting the church, killing many Christians. But our Lord Jesus cried from heaven, "Saul, Saul, why persecutest thou me?" (Acts 9:4). There is an unmistakable, radical, and holy self-centeredness about the Lord Jesus.

We can multiply examples. In John 8:58, He said, "Verily, verily, I say unto you, Before Abraham was, I am." In John 10:9, He said, "I am the door: by me if any man enter in, he shall be saved, and shall go in and out, and find pasture." In John 10:14, He said, "I am the good shepherd, and know my sheep, and am known of mine." In John 10:30, He said, "I and my Father are one." In Matthew 11:27, our Lord said, "All things are delivered unto me of my Father: and no man knoweth the Son, but the Father; neither knoweth any man the Father, save the Son, and he to whomsoever the Son will reveal him." In Luke 14:26, He said, "If any man come to me, and hate not his father, and mother, and wife, and children, and brethren, and sisters, yea, and his own life also, he cannot be my disciple." The devotion that Christ demands for Himself is much greater than the devotion we should have to anybody else, including our own fathers and mothers. Our dedication to even close relatives should look like hate compared to our commitment to Christ. This is precisely what Thomas Boston meant when he wrote this:

> In the evening, while I sat musing on what I had been preaching, viz. that the soul that has got a true discovery of Christ will be satisfied with Him alone, I proposed the question to myself, "Are you content with Christ alone? Would you be satisfied with Christ as your portion, even tho' there were no hell to be saved from?" And my soul answered, "Yes." I asked myself further, "Supposing that, would you be content in Him, if you were to lose credit and reputation and meet with trouble for His sake?"

Rev. Samuel Rutherford, with a Sketch of His Life by the Rev. A.A. Bonar (1891; repr., Edinburgh: Banner of Truth, 1984), 159.

My soul answered, "Yes. Such is my hatred of sin and love to Christ."[3]

Our Lord declared the necessity of such a radical and holy Christ-centeredness. As a result, if we cannot embrace the radical, holy, self-centeredness of Christ, we have not embraced biblical Christianity. This radical centrality of the person of Christ has escaped many who pretend to be interested in the teachings of Christianity. Whether it is a journalist, scholar, or the man on the street, most people want to know what the church's opinion is about this or that contemporary issue. What is the Christian view of homosexuality, cannabis, the growth of human trafficking, so-called same-sex marriage, and so on? They want to know the church's policy concerning a plethora of issues that they think are pressing and urgent.

In response, biblical Christians may reply, "My friend, with all due respect, who cares?" These other issues are trivial concerns if we have not addressed the most crucial question of life, which is, "Is Jesus who He said He is?" If the Lord Jesus is who He said He is, He is the authority on every other issue. Our respective opinions, feelings, or attitudes about anything are unimportant; if Jesus is indeed Lord, then eventually we must and will bow.

All debates about social or political issues are futile until we establish the criteria for deciding the right course of action. Where or what is our authority? Biblical Christianity says, "First things first: Who is this Jesus of Nazareth? Who is this person who dares to walk into a man's life and demand that the man abandon his career, change his worldview, reschedule his calendar, realign his relationships, and change his ambitions? Who is this Jesus who says to any of us in His crosshairs, 'Follow me'?" This is truly radical!

If Jesus is Lord of the entire universe, as He claimed, then we must get with His agenda. His agenda will be life for us because He is our creator and redeemer. Christianity is all about the Christ. He is the Word, the Logos, who was at the beginning with God and

---

[3]. Thomas Boston, *Memoirs of the Life, Times and Writings of the Reverend and Learned Thomas Boston A.M.* (1899; repr., Edinburgh: Banner of Truth, 1988), 61.

is Himself very God (see John 1:1–3). Worship Him, for in Him dwells all the fullness of the Godhead bodily (Col. 2:9), for He alone is the only begotten of the Father, full of grace and truth (John 1:14). Worship Him, for He is the lily of the valley, the bright and morning star, the fairest of ten thousand to our souls. Worship Him for He is altogether lovely and the lover of our souls; He is the only potentate, the King of Kings and Lord of Lords.

The Radical Call of Christ

There is a magnetic pull to the radical call of Christ, an attraction that compels true believers to rise and follow Him. It is a revolutionary, urgent call to respond to His own radical commitment to us, demonstrated in His mission of eternal redemption. It is an effectual call—though there may be some immediate pushback from the one who has been called, the forceful pull of Christ's call is ultimately irresistible. "And he arose, and followed him" (Matt. 9:9) is a summary statement, but that is all that is needed. The call was so radical and compelling that submission seemed to Matthew the only reasonable response.

We know from the revelation given to the prophet Isaiah, many centuries before the first advent of Jesus, that the magnetic pull of Christ's call would not take the form of outward attractiveness. The pull of Christ was not that He was handsome or charismatic in personality. According to Isaiah 53:2–3, the Suffering Servant, the Christ, would not be handsome, or a towering personage, or possess incredible charisma. Centuries later, the passion narrative of the Gospels shows us the Roman ruler, Pilate, laughing at the Christ with his sarcastic interrogation, "Art thou the King of the Jews?" (Mark 15:2). Likewise, Pilate asked the murderous mob, "Will ye that I release unto you the King of the Jews?" (Mark 15:9). He did not recognize the majesty of Christ; he mocked Him, saying, "Oh, this is Jesus Christ! I am quite surprised. He looks so insignificant, not at all like a king." Pilate was not impressed.

In contrast, Matthew heard a magnetic, compelling, and urgent call to radical action when he encountered Jesus. Christ commanded a kind of obedience from Matthew that was volitional yet nonetheless coercive. Matthew was in one sense free to resist, but at the same time he also felt forced to obey. Matthew processed the Lord's invitation and came to a decision, but, in a sense, he had no choice. The call required Matthew's consent, yet it was a totalitarian call.

In understanding this, the story of Mary and her alabaster box of ointment in John 12:1–8 may be helpful. Mary had taken an enormously expensive bottle of perfumed ointment, put it on our Lord Jesus's feet, and then wiped His feet with her hair. The other people in the room thought that this act was ridiculous. They said, in effect, "We have nothing against respecting the Lord Jesus, listening to His teaching, or supporting His healing ministry. But this is far too extravagant. What a waste!" We are even told that the thieving Judas Iscariot protested on behalf of the poor, whom he claimed would be more appropriate recipients of the money wasted in this act of worship by Mary. Of course, the text reminds us that Judas's true concern was finding more opportunities for theft (John 12:6).

Mary had heard the totalitarian call of Christ and realized that, with Jesus, it is all or nothing. She gave herself to Him completely, just as Matthew did when he resigned from his job. Our Lord Jesus defended her and her act of love. He said, "Let her alone: against the day of my burying hath she kept this" (John 12:7). That may seem to be a cryptic statement, but it was our Lord's way of making it clear that Mary understood that He would die for her. She sensed that our Lord was radically committed to her; she therefore had to respond by demonstrating her commitment to Him.

A true understanding of the active and passive obedience of Christ on our behalf is enough to make us rise and follow Him. Knowing that Christ kept the law perfectly, having lived the life that we should have lived, and having died the ultimate death, paying the price of our infinite debt of sin is enough to overwhelm any heart that the Holy Spirit has prepared. We become convinced that giving our all to Him is worth it when we understand that He gave His all for us. When we truly understand who has called us, we must get up, sell everything, take up our cross, and surrender everything to follow Him.

In Hebrews 10:5–7, we are reminded that our Lord Jesus Himself answered the call of God the Father in a similarly radical way. It is written there, "Wherefore when he cometh into the world, he saith, Sacrifice and offering thou wouldest not, but a body hast thou prepared me: in burnt offerings and sacrifices for sin thou hast had no pleasure. Then said I, Lo, I come (in the volume of the book it is written of me,) to do thy will, O God." God the Father called our Lord Jesus, God the Son, and our Lord said, "Here am I. Send Me." Whatever it costs for us to rise and follow the totalitarian call of Christ without reservation is nothing compared to what it cost Christ to atone for our sin. The Lord Jesus stood between sinners and eternal destruction and took the wrath of divine justice upon Himself for us. He endured the most blatant mockery and humiliation for us. His obedience in the incarnation, His holy life, and His humiliation to the point of death on the cross demand that we get up with a radical commitment to follow and worship Him.

Left to ourselves, we are neither brave nor courageous in the face of pain, discomfort, and terror. We generally prefer to take the line of least resistance and to run away from the smallest threat to our comfort or happiness. But when we think of His goodness and what He has done for us, our souls cry, "Hallelujah!" and we start to reason, "This is the least I can do. I must rise, take up my cross, and follow Him. Such selflessness deserves my fullest service." With the hymn writer, we affirm,

> My life, my love, I give to Thee,
> Thou Lamb of God who died for me;
> Oh, may I ever faithful be,
> My Savior and my God!
>
> I'll live for Him who died for me,
> How happy then my life shall be!
> I'll live for Him who died for me,
> My Savior and my God!

I now believe Thou dost receive,
For Thou hast died that I might live;
And now henceforth I'll trust to Thee,
My Savior and my God!

Oh, Thou who died on Calvary,
To save my soul and make me free;
I'll consecrate my life to Thee,
My Savior and my God![4]

---

4. R.E. Hudson, "I'll Live for Him," 1882.

Chapter 2

RADICAL TRANSFORMATION

The Westminster Shorter Catechism reminds us, "Man's chief end is to glorify God, and to enjoy Him forever" (WSC 1). This stress on the centrality of God's glory in everything is thoroughly biblical. Indeed, the primary teaching of John 12 is that everything God has done, everything He is doing, and everything God ever will do is to show us His glory. God is the source of all glory, and to Him alone belongs the glory.

Such talk may seem rather esoteric to the average person, who asks what the glory of God has to do with them and how it affects their everyday life. Yet at the time of the Protestant Reformation in the sixteenth century, there was a momentous recalibration of the church's understanding of our salvation, which included a renewed understanding that our salvation must be according to the Holy Scriptures alone, through faith alone, by grace alone, in Christ alone, and to the glory of God alone. This emphasis on God's glory led to an overflow of doxology in truly biblical churches, singing enthusiastically, "Thee, O God, we praise."[1]

The Hebrew word for "glory" (*kabod*) originally meant physical heaviness or weight; as a result, it also came to represent that which is essential, substantial, and of lasting significance. A thing of glory will not be easily moved—it is not flimsy, shallow, or weightless. Ultimately, every culture and individual must grapple with what we will glorify. We all embrace certain abiding values and priorities;

---

1. In Latin, this phrase is *Te Deum Laudamus*, the name of one of the classic hymns from the early history of the church.

these in turn determine what we think should be retained or canceled from our history and civilization, what we work toward, and what we are willing to sacrifice for and defend. Our lives cannot be lived with any semblance of peace and stability if we cannot decide what we consider to be the weighty matters of existence, the things that deserve glory.

Our generation assumes that such matters can be decided by societal consensus. As a result, we live in a culture increasingly committed to the notions that there are no absolute values, that our origins are accidental and without purpose, that our future is a journey into nothing, and that the best we can do in the meantime is to create meaning for and by ourselves. It is, of course, absurd to argue that we came from nothing and are headed to nothing, but we can still attempt to make something meaningful out of life right now by attributing glory to essentially meaningless objects and activities. These self-manufactured "values" and "rights" are arbitrary and subject to being dismissed or reversed by whoever has the power in a given context. The philosopher Nietzsche saw clearly that if there is no God, it does not matter whether we live a life of kindness or violence. In that case, everything is ultimately weightless and undeserving of glory.

Our generation has very little respect for the notion that the creator of the universe has already interpreted reality for us. Yet a meaningful life for us is to respect and intelligently reflect His image in us on all matters of life and living. We are created to be like God in a way that is true of no other creatures. God made human beings alone to bear His image and likeness. This means that all human beings have a special honor and value that is not duplicated in any other aspect of creation. People have been set in the world to display the true and living God's glory and establish His will on earth. We have the blessing and responsibility to proclaim the lordship of Christ in our environment and culture, not least by spreading the word of the glorious gospel.

There is almost universal resistance in our time to the idea that we live under the authority of a sovereign ruler to whom we must all account and to whom we must give all the glory. Yet it should be evident to every honest observer that past generations' experiments at finding an alternative consensus have not ended well. It is also apparent that our present generation's politically correct orientation has only polarized us more than ever before. Our contemporary revisionist reading of history has put us on a trajectory toward the ultimate showdown between totalitarianism and the freedoms that we have enjoyed in the West.

There is an alternative—we may find a lasting center for our society in pursuing the glory of God. There is hope in affirming that all glory comes from God, all significance comes from God, all lasting value comes from God, and that everything is weightless without God. According to Acts 17:28, "For in him we live, and move, and have our being; as certain also of your own poets have said, For we are also his offspring." We all know in our hearts that the suggestion that we are adrift in a sea of relativism is utter nonsense. None of us can accept that everything is weightless and without meaning, for God has placed the knowledge of Himself within our hearts (Rom. 1:19). That is why the experiment at pursuing consensus without reference to God, while admittedly very tempting, inevitably ends in utter futility.

Deep down, we all yearn for glory, and we all seem to know that none of us are qualified to define it. Despite what the culture tells us, we still find ourselves asking what should get glory in our lives, as if it is built into who we are to expect to learn of this glory from above, from our maker. Humans constantly need to reaffirm their identity and the source of their significance and security. Whatever the label, all religions of human works propose that we find our identity, significance, and security in ourselves and our own best efforts. In contrast, biblical Christianity says that is all vanity. Biblical Christianity insists that we continue to sing, "On Christ the solid Rock I stand, all other ground is sinking sand."[2] It maintains that we were

---

2. Edward Mote, "My Hope is Built on Nothing Less," 1834.

never intended to find our identity, significance, and security in any other source than the God of the Bible.

John 12:27–36 is a pivotal passage that addresses this matter, helping us to know whether we are genuinely saved and radically transformed or not. These words of our Lord Jesus show us how we experience God's glory or, better, whether we have experienced God's glory at all.

The Weight of God's Significance

One of the things that happens when we experience the glory of God is that an overwhelming sense of God's significance consumes us. This fact is demonstrated clearly in John 12:27–28, where Jesus says, "Now is my soul troubled; and what shall I say? Father, save me from this hour: but for this cause came I unto this hour. Father, glorify thy name. Then came there a voice from heaven, saying, I have both glorified it, and will glorify it again."

Our Lord Jesus's experience of God's glory, though essentially different from ours because of His divine nature, informs our experience of the glory of God. When we experience the glory of God, we recognize Him as the essential being and principle in our lives—nothing matters but Him. Everything in our lives is defined and prioritized by Him. Every aspect of our being now oozes with doxology, and we joyfully join the psalmist in singing, "Not unto us, O Lord, not unto us, but unto thy name give glory, for thy mercy, and for thy truth's sake. Wherefore should the heathen say, Where is now their God? But our God is in the heavens: he hath done whatsoever he hath pleased" (Ps. 115:1–3).

This theme is echoed throughout the Holy Scriptures. The chief end of our God, and our Lord Jesus, is to manifest and enjoy His glory. God is about His own glory—this is what He is after. As a result, when we are truly saved, this also becomes our chief end. The distinguishing mark of a true disciple of Christ is that they have experienced the glory of God and now delight to glorify Him. This is what separates them from the rest of humanity.

When we experience the glory of God, the weight of God's significance overwhelms us. If the God of the Bible, the Lord Jesus Christ, has not emerged as the consuming passion and priority of our lives, then we have likely not met Christ. For this reason, our Lord Jesus prayed to the Father in John 17:22, "And the glory which thou gavest me I have given them; that they may be one, even as we are one." In the same way, the apostle Paul said, "For God, who commanded the light to shine out of darkness, hath shined in our hearts, to give the light of the knowledge of the glory of God in the face of Jesus Christ" (2 Cor. 4:6). The same apostle also wrote in Colossians 1:27, "To whom God would make known what is the riches of the glory of this mystery among the Gentiles; which is Christ in you, the hope of glory." All true disciples of Christ have this in common. Their relationship with Christ is the defining principle, the focus and foundation of their lives.

What we speak of here is not necessarily a vision of some kind of mystical light. Throughout history, some people have physically seen the glory of God like Moses at the burning bush (Exodus 3) or the fourth man in the fiery furnace with the three young Hebrew men (Daniel 3), but that is not the essence of the experience we are describing. Remember that *glory* refers to weighty, substantial, and significant things. There are cases where much drama, mystery, and bright light are associated with this glory in the Holy Scriptures, but these are not necessary or normative to it. At its core, it is an experience in which God's power and sovereignty capture and captivate the human heart. Worship becomes our favorite activity. Gazing by faith on the person of Christ, beholding His glory, and contemplating His work become the longing of our souls. Christ can no longer be merely a part of our lives; He Himself is our life.

The business of the Christian life is to boast every day—not about ourselves, but about the Lord. This boasting forms the content of our doxology. This showing off is the motivation for our acts of charity and gospel ventures. The apostle Paul testified in these terms when he wrote, "But God forbid that I should glory, save in the cross of our Lord Jesus Christ, by whom the world is crucified unto me, and I unto the world" (Gal. 6:14). We know when this glory has invaded us because we suddenly find ourselves running away from the limelight, not out of a false sense of modesty, but so that the spotlight will be on Christ alone. Suddenly, we are ready to endure abuse, willing to face contempt and derision, and prepared to suffer loss if it means that Christ may be magnified. We must decrease, and Christ must increase, for He alone is altogether lovely, He alone is the wisdom and power of God, He alone has the cattle on a thousand hills, and He alone is the Ancient of Days (see John 3:30). We testify with the hymn writer:

> Jesus is all the world to me,
> And true to Him I'll be;
> Oh, how could I this friend deny,
> When He's so true to me?
> Following Him, I know I'm right,
> He watches o'er me day and night;
> Following Him by day and night,
> He's my friend.[3]

We know that we have experienced the glory of God when the weight of God's significance consumes us. Those who are not Christians may be consumed by the weight of their own significance, but in reality, they are featherweights pretending to be heavyweights. True Christians have settled the question about what they must do with their life. They affirm the apostle Paul's admonition, "And whatsoever ye do in word or deed, do all in the name of the Lord Jesus, giving thanks to God and the Father by him" (Col. 3:17).

Because of the remarkable and majestic entrance of Christ in our lives, we are now embarrassed when our names are praised, for we know the truly deserving name which is above every name (Phil. 2:9–11). We are embarrassed when our performance is eulogized, for we are counting on nothing but the imputed righteousness of Christ. We are resistant when the abomination of a so-called sacrament of penance is suggested, for "nothing in [our] hand[s] [we]

---

3. Will L. Thompson, "Jesus is All the World to Me," 1904.

bring, simply to the cross [we] cling."[4] We know better when someone informs us that *Jehovahjireh* (the Lord provides) is about our right to material prosperity, for we understand that it is about a ram in the thicket, the Lamb of God who takes away the sin of the world (see Gen. 22:14; John 1:29). We are now embarrassed by our own wicked excursions in idolatry, acting like the dog who has returned to his vomit (Prov. 26:11), only to be reminded that in Christ is all the fullness of the Godhead bodily (Col. 2:9). We are now saddened by our feeble and lethargic worship, for in Christ Jesus, we have the one who is the center of all things, beside whom, in the final analysis, nothing and no one else matters.

The Wonder of God's Sacrifice

We have attempted to explain the epiphany that true believers experience concerning God's majestic presence and significance in their lives. But the catalyst for such an experience is always the cross of Jesus Christ. What drives us to recognize God's supremacy, importance, sovereignty, and unavoidable dominance in our lives? It is the old rugged cross. John's gospel makes this plain: "The people therefore, that stood by, and heard it, said that it thundered: others said, An angel spake to him. Jesus answered and said, This voice came not because of me, but for your sakes. Now is the judgment of this world: now shall the prince of this world be cast out. And I, if I be lifted up from the earth, will draw all men unto me. This he said, signifying what death he should die" (John 12:29–33). This fact is very surprising to our generation, and perhaps to every generation. It seems strange that a Roman crucifixion's horror, abuse, and inhumanity should now become the epitome of glory. Yet it is indeed so.

In our Lord Jesus's ministry, there were three times in which the Father spoke directly from heaven: His baptism (Matt. 3:17), His transfiguration (Matt. 17:5), and this passage in John 12. Here, for the disciples' benefit (v. 30), the Father placed His seal of approval upon our Lord Jesus's mediatorial work, especially the atoning

---

4. Augustus Toplady, "Rock of Ages," 1776.

sacrifice. According to verse 27, this was always His purpose—He came to earth to die. The cross was not merely a symbol of sacrificial caring for others, it was the payment of an infinite debt with infinitely valuable blood, the blood of God incarnate. When our Lord Jesus bore the penal wrath of God for sinners and overcame the power of death, He terminated the power of sin over Adam's race (see Rom. 5:12–19). This vicarious act is where we learn what true glory looks like.

The Holy Scriptures teach us that if we want to see the glory of God, we must go to the cross of Calvary. This does not mean there is no evidence of the glory of God elsewhere; far from it. Psalm 19:1 declares, "The heavens declare the glory of God; and the firmament sheweth his handywork." There is no doubt that the natural world around us testifies to and manifests the glory of God, but this is a mere reflection. It is indirect glory, as the light of the moon reflects the greater glory of the sun. But when we go to the cross, it is as if we look directly at the sun. The blaze is unbearable.

If we want to understand and experience the glory of God, we have to see the glory of God in the cross. We not only have to *believe* that the Lord Jesus died for us, but we also have to *glory* in that death. To glory in something is to count it as the essential thing in our lives and adjust every other agenda to support, defend, and promote it. A genuine Christian has accepted that this death of Christ is the defining principle of their life, the basis of their identity, significance, and security. There is nothing else in life that comes close to this. Unless the cross of Calvary is writ large in our lives, we have no legitimate claim to experiencing the glory of God.

In the cross, we see the justice of God and the love of God glorified simultaneously. Many today struggle with the doctrine that the God of the Bible is both love and wrath, just as the ancient heretic Marcion did. They wrestle with the reality that He is both the light of hope *and* a consuming fire (John 8:12; Heb. 12:29), but a true believer has been given a glorious appreciation of how it is possible for God to be both just and the justifier of the ungodly (Rom. 4:5).

Once we understand the cross, we begin to understand how the gospel works.

Our Lord Jesus testified in John 12:27 that His soul was so troubled about the suffering that lay ahead of Him that He felt the very human impulse to abandon His mission. Our Lord Jesus was and is truly divine, so the mission of redemption could never be postponed or canceled. But He was and is also truly human, and the agony that found expression in His words was inevitable. The prospect that intimidated the Lord Jesus Christ, the second person of the Trinity, the eternal Son of God, in His human nature was beginning to feel the weight of our sins and anticipating the full wrath of God the Father falling on His head. This explains why, in the heat of the crucifixion, He quoted Psalm 22:1, "My God, my God, why hast thou forsaken me?" (see Matt. 27:46).

Our Lord Jesus faced the ultimate punishment on behalf of sinners like us. The most profound penalty for sin is to be cast out, separated, and utterly ignored by the only person whose love can fulfill us. We all have an idea of what that is like, though on a lesser scale. At some time or other, we all have been rejected by someone we desperately desired to accept and celebrate us. We know what alienation and emotional coldness feel like. But what we have experienced is nothing compared to the cosmic alienation that our Lord Jesus experienced. He faced the worst fate that anyone could ever face when He drank the cup of the full wrath of God. He experienced nothing less than hell itself on Calvary.

It was not just the physical torture Christ endured on the cross that is significant, great though it was. Of far greater significance is the utter rejection of being cast out and forsaken. Only when we grasp the lengths to which our God went to rescue us at Calvary will we genuinely worship this true and living God and understand why gazing on Christ should become the consuming passion of our lives. This is the fullest experience of the glory of God.

When we see the beauty of what Christ did on the cross of Calvary through the eyes of faith, we find that we can never get over it. The transcendent splendor of the energies of the matchless sacrifice of Christ draws us like a magnet. We can now see the depth of our own sin, the magnitude of the holiness of God, the power of His justice, and the magnitude of our Lord's sacrifice (and we recognize that He did that for us personally). Glorying in that matchless death makes us see that nothing is more important than our God.

The Worthlessness of God-Substitutes

We must now get practical about this matter. How specifically do we glory in the cross? Whatever we glory in is the boast of our lives, the thing that we celebrate the most. We all know how to boast and brag—such boasting is dangerous because it is often a narcissistic, self-righteous celebration of ourselves. Instead, the Lord Jesus must be the focus of our boasting. No other object of faith is worthy of our worship. We become idol worshipers if Christ is not the solitary object of our devotion and doxology. We are deep in spiritual adultery if we are not constantly gazing on Christ. There is no coming to Christ or walking with Christ without a conscious and determined jettisoning of every idolatrous obsession or expression in our lives.

We have already looked at Galatians 6:14, where Paul wrote, "But God forbid that I should glory, save in the cross of our Lord Jesus Christ, by whom the world is crucified unto me, and I unto the world." The apostle had learned that boasting in the cross meant that he had to stop boasting about everything else, including himself. We glory in the cross when we see the worthlessness of every substitute for God that we have erected in our lives and commence a search-and-destroy mission for every manifestation of the same. We are glorying in the cross when we identify the things in our lives that compete with God—the things that we glory in and boast about—and destroy them, one by one.

We will never experience the glory of God until we break down our idols. Nor will we continue to experience the glory of God unless we are committed to the task of destroying the idols that continue to emerge in our lives. The truth is that we must never find our identity, significance, and security in anyone or anything but Christ.

So, let us go ahead and boast to our hearts' content. However, we will not boast in our own choices, but in our Father's choice of us from before the foundation of the world. We will not boast in our sacrifices but in Christ's sacrifice on the old, rugged cross. We will not boast in our birth and pedigree but in the new birth from above by the power of the Holy Spirit. We will not boast in our giftedness and blessings but in the giver and the blesser of our lives. We will not boast in our obedience but in the active and passive obedience of Christ. We will not boast in our piety but in the merits of Christ alone. Christ, and Christ alone, must have all the glory.

Chapter 3

RADICAL WORSHIP

Contemporary worship is all over the place. We do not speak merely geographically—rather, we refer to our generation's confusion concerning what worship should be. We see worship services where people are encouraged to laugh uncontrollably, when no joke was uttered or the humor was inappropriate. This is supposed to be Spirit-induced laughter, but it is a blasphemous association with the Holy Spirit. We see theatrical displays of faked healings in the context of worship, while the so-called healers refuse to visit the local hospitals to utilize their supposed giftedness. We see huge congregations celebrating the contemporary cult of the self, listening with rapt attention to teaching that resembles life coaching, and which affirms the "mystical power" within each human being. To all this, the contemporary celebrity preachers add a few out-of-context Bible verses and big smiles, along with sensual religious lyrics and slick music.

Large crowds of people seem hungry for this nonsense, and marketing consultants seem convinced that if local churches and worshiping communities are to grow, they cannot stick to biblical methods—rather, they must embrace what this generation demands and desires if they are going to survive. But biblical Christians must challenge this nonsense with the unadulterated Word of God. We believe that the Bible teaches the regulative principle of worship, whereby we only allow in worship what God has explicitly commanded in Holy Scripture. We are not free to offer anything we wish to God, provided it is not explicitly forbidden. God has not left us in the dark about how to worship Him. This position may not be popular with the masses, but the church of the Lord Jesus Christ can be assured that "the gates of hell shall not prevail against it" (Matt. 16:18).

If our chief desire is to glorify God alone, as we argued in the last chapter, then how we worship God will matter to us. We do not simply come to church to receive answers to our prayers or wisdom to face the most complicated problems of our lives. Worship is not ultimately about us and our needs; it is about coming into the presence of the living God.

Psalm 95—which is sometimes called the *Venite* after its opening words in Latin, "O Come"—gives us a concise summary of the priorities of worshiping the true and living God. Throughout the centuries, believers in Christ have looked to this psalm for guidance on the worship of our God. This powerful psalm makes it abundantly clear that worshiping the living God with integrity demands involvement that is fully engaged, denounces idolatry, and submits to the imperatives of Scripture.

Worship Demands Involvement That Is Fully Engaged

When we worship, our goal is to ascribe supreme value to our God in a manner that energizes and engages every aspect of our being, including our mind, emotions, and will. We see this truth reflected in the three imperatives in Psalm 95 (vv. 1, 6, 8). In verse 1, the psalmist challenges worshipers to worship God with their emotions: "O come, let us sing unto the LORD: let us make a joyful noise to the rock of our salvation." In verse 6, we are called to worship God with our wills: "O come, let us worship and bow down: let us kneel before the LORD our maker." Meanwhile, in verse 8, the psalmist addresses our thinking and understanding: "Harden not your heart, as in the provocation, and as in the day of temptation in the wilderness."

Worship engages all our faculties—the mind, the emotions, and the will. Our entire being is involved. If we are merely enamored with beautiful ceremonies and rituals that we repeat thoughtlessly, even if the content is doctrinally sound and theologically rich, it is not authentic worship. Authentic worship takes place when we are ravished by the beauty of God and find joy in Him. Of course, the opposite extreme is also true. We can participate in a worship service so profound that it drives us to tears, but if our lifestyle, character, and behavioral patterns remain unchanged, then that too is inauthentic worship. It may be a cultural experience, or an emotional experience, or even an aesthetic experience, but we cannot call it biblical worship. True worship entails the entire being.

That engagement of the psalmist's whole being comes from him surveying and taking an inventory of the excellencies and wonders of the being of God. After the imperatives of verses 1–2, the next verses begin with the key word *for*: "For the LORD is a great God, and a great King above all gods. In his hand are the deep places of the earth: the strength of the hills is his also" (vv. 3–4); "For he is our God; and we are the people of his pasture, and the sheep of his hand" (v. 7). The psalmist is carefully measuring and evaluating God's nature and His attributes. He is scrutinizing them and reflecting upon them until they reverberate in his mind. A cursory glance will not do—the Holy One of Israel deserves his undivided attention. All the faculties of the psalmist are engaged until he has squeezed the last drop of juice out of the fruit of the glorious attributes of God.

Familiarity often eclipses the beauty all around us. We miss the significance of many things that are right under our noses. Our God is so near, but because of our sin, He is so far. Yet with a focused meditation that engages all our faculties, we are able to have a fresh look at our God. We are driven to rediscover that He is indeed altogether lovely. We come to appreciate the incalculable value of His holy person, and we are astounded. We realize that we have not been living on the basis of the treasure that we have in Him. Because our sinful familiarity and hardened profanity have eclipsed God's beauty, we naturally cannot grasp the true significance of a covenant relationship with our God. But when, by His grace, we are made to see it afresh, our entire life is transformed and invigorated. This gets to the heart of worshiping with integrity. The modern English word *worship* comes from the Old English *worth-ship*. In other words, to worship God is to see clearly what He is worth and to live in a manner that is worthy of Him.

Many in the West claim to believe in God, yet they are practical atheists. Their belief has no impact on their lives. They may pray to God sometimes, but their spirituality is divorced from the demands of Christ. They think of God in a manner that leaves them utterly unaffected by biblical Christianity's soteriological and ethical implications. They are entirely unaware of the treasure that is our God, and as a result, they never truly worship Him. Indeed, each of us needs to examine ourselves to see if we have ever truly worshiped Him in this way.

Worship Denounces Idolatry

The reason many people get involved in merely formal, thoughtless, and passionless worship exercises is found in verse 3 of the psalm where the conflict between the real God and our designer gods is described, "For the LORD is a great God, and a great King above all gods" (Ps. 95:3). We do not worship the true and living God with integrity because we are often worshiping something else already. Our problem with authentic worship is that we often ascribe ultimate value to something that is not the true and living God.

The world is not simply divided into people who worship and those who do not. On the contrary, everybody worships—even atheists. The world is divided into people who worship lesser things and those who worship the only object worthy of worship, the God of the Bible. Those are our only alternatives. And if we ascribe ultimate value to the wrong things, our view of reality will be fundamentally distorted.

We will only be able to worship the true and living God with integrity if we are prepared to admit that our hearts have already ascribed ultimate value to something else or someone else, to that which is temporal—that is, our worship is instinctively focused in the wrong place. To worship with integrity, we must commit ourselves to place ultimate value on the true and living God. Every one of us has, at some point, put our hope in something or someone other than the God of the Bible, hoping that this alternative god will give us significance, security, and form the basis of our identity. We hope and believe that our idols will make us happy and fulfilled, and so we submit ourselves to their demands.

Whatever controls us is our lord and master. If we are not controlled by the true and living God, someone or something else will fill the gap; there will be a substitute deity, an idolatrous replacement. If we are motivated by a desire for power and control, we will be controlled and consumed by manipulation and influence peddling. If we live for acceptance by other people, we will be controlled by the people we try to impress. One thing is certain: we do not control ourselves. We are governed by whatever idol we create and bow to.

If we have difficulty identifying the particular god we worship, we merely have to ask ourselves a few simple questions: "What is it that I live for? What do I depend on? What do I desperately desire? What am I so afraid of losing? What is it that drives me crazy when it all goes wrong?" Our answers to these questions will tell us the actual objects of our worship, the things to which we have attributed supreme value. Our loyalty is divided, which prevents us from authentic worship of the true and living God.

Our ultimate problem is always what or whom we worship. It is only when we see that God's love is more satisfying, more valuable, and more beautiful than any other kind of love that we will stop living in fear over our relationships. Only when we see that God's honor and the corresponding relationship with Him are more beautiful and powerful than any other form of honor or pleasure that we will stop going into a tailspin whenever we are criticized or failing. Emotional drama, anxiety, despondency, nervousness, and the fear of what people think are often the result of bowing to a false god in our lives. Nothing less than reassigning the ultimate value of our life from where it is to the true and living God will heal us, change us, and make us truly happy.

Worshiping with integrity is thus much more than just showing up and doing our duty to God. We must come to grips with the fact that we have illegitimately assigned ultimate value to the wrong thing and must repent of this. Transformation occurs as we sing God's praises, read and listen to His Word, pray responsible prayers, and participate in the church's two ordinances (baptism and the Lord's Supper). Gradually and incrementally, through these divinely prescribed means of grace, we are healed and begin to be weaned off those things that control and dominate us, creating room for the God of the Bible, the only one whose worship will not distort our lives.

As we worship, our hearts look progressively more toward Christ. We begin to reassign the ultimate value to the one who will truly satisfy us. The Lord is the only God who is a shepherd. We are the sheep of His pasture, the flock of His hand (Ps. 95:7). He is the only God who forgives His people. He is the only God who has died to pay for the damage that we have done. This God is worthy of our worship, and as we worship Him, we are gradually made whole.

Worship Submits to Biblical Requirements

There are at least four requirements in Psalm 95 that are essential to authentic worship. These are the necessity of covenant community, concrete convictions, celestial communion, and continual calmness. We will examine each of these in turn.

The necessity of covenant community for proper worship should be obvious, but many people miss it in reading this psalm. The whole psalm is written in the plural. *We* are called to worship in a covenant community. That does not mean that individual worship is unimportant. Our own personal ability to praise God in private is vital. In many ways, individual worship is a prelude to and preparation for corporate worship, which God designed to be the pivotal transforming experience in the believer's life.

While there is a place for private communion with God, it is in the covenant community that our character, gifts, challenges, and relational skills are best exposed and addressed. Our interactions with various personalities in the covenant community draw out our entire personalities. No one individual can draw out the whole essence. We will only see the multi-dimensional nature of our characters in the context of community. This goes against our contemporary Western understanding of spirituality. Yet Hebrews 10:25 also reminds us of the indispensability of community: "Not forsaking the assembling of ourselves together, as the manner of some is; but exhorting one another: and so much the more, as ye see the day approaching." We will never know God as He is unless we are regularly involved in a disciplined worshiping community.

This is the only way to get an accurate vision of God; it cannot be achieved simply through one-on-one time with God. Just like children need parents and family, believers need pastors and the covenant community. A personal devotional life, though meaningful, will not show you all of the facets of an enduring life with God. The more diverse the persons who make up our worshiping community, the better it is for each member. The more we have young and old, male and female, of all generations, races, and socioeconomic classes worshiping together, the better it is for all of us. Being among those who have bonded around the gospel of Christ is the best context in which to begin to heal the breaches that divide the human race and to bridge the gaps between cultures, races, and classes of people. If our worship is to have integrity, we need the covenant community.

Authentic worship also needs to be founded on truth, in the shape of concrete convictions about who God is and who we ourselves are before Him. Ephesians 4:14 admonishes us, "That we henceforth be no more children, tossed to and fro, and carried about with every wind of doctrine, by the sleight of men, and cunning craftiness, whereby they lie in wait to deceive." There needs to be an anchor for our thinking in the truth, if we are not to be tossed around by every turbulent cultural trend.

How does the psalmist know that God is a shepherd? How does he know that God is our God and the one who has given Himself to us? How does he know that we are the people of His pasture and the flock under His care? The answer is simple. The psalmist has embraced and submitted to what the inspired authors of Scripture have said about God. The psalmist is committed to the Bible as the self-revelation of God, wherein he may find accurately laid out the excellencies of our God, which drive his worship.

Those who resist the notion of biblical revelation as the basis of truth only create more significant problems for themselves. For instance, if you are not willing to submit to the truth of Scripture as the self-revelation of God, then you have to design your own truth and create a god in your own image. This necessarily cuts you off from any ability to have a genuine spiritual experience. The god you have designed is totally under your control, so that it will never challenge or correct your thinking. How can you have an authentic relationship with a personally designed puppet? You are pulling the strings, playing an idolatrous game with yourself. What is more, this delusion will isolate you from those around you. If everyone designs their god and their own truth, there is no basis for community because no one has anything in common.

Authentic worship also requires celestial communion or, to put it more simply, the presence of God. If God is absent, what is the point in going to church? After all, the purpose of worship is to come into His presence and kneel before Him (see Ps. 95:6). Some people are uncomfortable talking about God's tangible presence in our midst. God is present everywhere, they remind us. Psalm 139:7 says, "Whither shall I go from thy spirit? or whither shall I flee from thy presence?" They wish to leave it at that. But David says to the Lord in Psalm 51:11, "Cast me not away from thy presence; and take not thy holy spirit from me." The prophet Isaiah pleads with the Lord, "Oh that thou wouldest rend the heavens, that thou wouldest come down, that the mountains might flow down at thy presence" (Isa. 64:1). Even though God is everywhere, there are nonetheless special times of worship during which the Holy Spirit will make you personally aware of the very presence of God. You will sense His palpable reality. Our expectation and goal in authentic worship should thus always be to come into God's presence and know His love.

Finally, there is continual calmness, which refers to the peace and tranquility that comes from the gospel, the Sabbath rest that endures (Heb. 4:9). This otherwise upbeat psalm ends on a rather somber note, reminding Israel of their unbelief in the desert. When the children of Israel left their bondage in Egypt and were on their way to the promised land, they looked forward to the rest and peace that they would receive when they arrived there. But their immediate circumstances involved living in tents in the desert, and they were restless for their future home. All they had to go on was the promise of that rest that would come when they lived in a land flowing with milk and honey (Ex. 3:8).

Even though many of them did not make it into the promised land due to their stubbornness and unbelief (see Num. 13–14), we know that Joshua finally got the children of Israel into the promised land. They experienced some semblance of rest when they took possession of their inheritance. But what is very interesting is how the New Testament addresses this rest. An entire chapter, Hebrews 4, focuses on how Psalm 95 ends. The author of Hebrews asks why David in Psalm 95 would warn worshipers not to miss the Sabbath rest of God when Joshua had already guided the people into the promised land. The answer is that the physical rest that the children of Israel experienced must be pointing to a more profound rest that is still available for us, and that we too can miss if we are not careful. Just as God rested from His creation work on the seventh day (see Gen. 1:1–2:3), in the gospel, we spiritually rest from our tainted and insufficient works of righteousness. We are delivered from the futility of offering to God what amounts to nothing but filthy rags (Isa. 64:6).

The message of the book of Hebrews is that Jesus Christ came to earth and lived a perfect life in our place as our substitute. He then died the death we should have died because of our infinite debt of sin. He took hell for us when He endured the cross of Calvary. Because of this substitutionary death, we can relax. Our salvation rests on the finished work of another, not on our own best efforts. Embracing this truth with all our hearts leads us to continual calmness—that is, rest.

False religions say the opposite. They all shout, "Get up! You have work to do to appease God. You can never have the assurance that you are in the clear. You have to balance the scales of justice all by yourself. Make that pilgrimage. Do those rituals. Say the prayers we have prescribed. Be obedient! Jump through our religious hoops. If you live a good enough life, God might bless you." Their message is a prescription for tiredness and despair. We will never attain rest this way.

But there is a better way in the gospel of Jesus Christ. There is rest for the people of God, an eternal Sabbath rest. Our God has given us in Jesus Christ a perfect record that we receive by faith. If you believe the gospel, you rest from your work spiritually. That means you do not have to jump through any more hoops to be loved and accepted by God. You do not have to be perfect. You do not have to be the brightest Bible student or theologian. You do not have to be the best servant or missionary for the kingdom. You do not have to give the most in the community of faith. Jesus has done it for you, in your place.

Many of us have been working ourselves to death all our lives to prove to everyone that we belong, that we are significant, and that we are deserving of some semblance of security. Finally, we can rest in the gospel, experiencing the constant calmness that comes by grace alone, through faith alone, and in Christ alone. This is a sweet, satisfying, authentic, enduring, and eternal rest. This is a rest where we take our burdens to the cross and leave them there, where we cast all our cares on Jesus, and where we find relief on our march to Zion, for in the midst of our exertion, we see that it is He who carries us (Isa. 40:29–31).

Chapter 4

RADICAL PRAYER

Christianity emphasizes the priority and indispensability of prayer in all its expressions. It is a fact that devout believers everywhere pray. None of us can make a case for spiritual vitality where there is no passion for or persistence in prayer. It is also a fact that the efficacy of prayer has always been questioned. Is anyone listening to our prayers, and does He answer (or even care)?

The narrative of Genesis 18:16–33 gives a compelling demonstration of prayer that should inform the praying of all believers. Radical prayer is within the grasp of every true disciple of Christ. This is important because underestimating the power of prayer along with misunderstanding the biblical purpose and mechanics of prayer have been to a large extent behind the spiritual declension of our generation.

This narrative singles out a particular event in the life of the patriarch Abraham that addresses the matter of prayer. At the beginning of Genesis 18, three men came to the door of Abraham's tent, and Abraham welcomed them (Gen. 18:1–2). Ancient Near Eastern hospitality was such that it was a person's duty to welcome, accommodate, and feed travelers; there were no inns or hotels at which they might stay. During the meal, through extraordinary spiritual discernment, it became clear to Abraham that one of those three men was the Lord God Himself in human guise—a theophany. When the three men got up to leave, Abraham went with them (18:16), and the subsequent passage records for us the dialogue between Abraham and God, which provides a model for our prayers.

Prayer Initiated by the Mediation of God

An essential prerequisite to prayer is often missed in our generation—Abraham did not take the initiative. Verses 17 and 18 tell us that it was the Lord who turned and said, "Shall I hide from Abraham that thing which I do; seeing that Abraham shall surely become a great and mighty nation, and all the nations of the earth shall be blessed in him?" No one says aloud, "Should I tell so and so about this?" unless there is a strong desire to do so. It is God who began the dialogue. Abraham's prayer was thus a response to God's speech. It did not begin with Abraham talking; it started with God speaking. That is how radical prayer works. Radical prayer is properly a response to divine revelation. Without being informed by the content of divine revelation, our prayers are likely to be shallow, foolish, and pretentious. Radical, efficacious prayer involves reaching out to God as He really is, not as we imagine or would prefer Him to be.

If we pray to God as we hope He is, we create a god in our own image, which is self-worship. We are praying to a projection of ourselves. That is an assault on the first two commandments of the Decalogue. The first tells us to worship God alone, and the second tells us that we should not offer up any improper worship to God (Ex. 20:3–6). We are to offer only what He has specifically prescribed. It may be comfortable for us to serve gods that never contradict us or make inconvenient demands on us. The deities that we create are essentially bellhops or servants—such gods exist to serve us, not the other way around. The God of the Bible, however, the true and living God, commands obedience, worship, and the preeminence of His holy interests. He does indeed help us with our concerns, but ultimately that is so we may more effectively bow and serve Him and Him alone.

The truth is that designer gods are highly overrated. They promise far more than they can deliver. Such gods cannot speak, or move, or have any impact on events around us, because behind the mask there is nothing more than ourselves—it is self-worship. The true and living God acts differently because He invites us to have a real relationship with Him. He will push back when we talk and act foolishly. The real God will contradict us, for He has a will and a written Word that will cross our desires and tell us things we hate or do not want to hear.

Anyone who reads the Bible seriously will sooner or later run into something that offends them. That is because such Bible readers deal with reality in each scriptural encounter. The real God is not just a projection of our personalities—He is not someone or something we have made up or invented. We did not make Him, neither can we make Him do anything, for it is He who has made us. He alone has the right to challenge us to be conformed to His holy will and purposes. He is God, after all.

The God of the Bible comes to us and speaks to us in His Word. That is authentic spirituality. God's Word must inform our prayers. This is how Abraham prays in Genesis 18—he hears God speak, and his prayer is a response to what he has heard. Authentic spirituality is not calling into the void, "Lord, I need you. Are you out there?" On the contrary, radical prayer begins with responding to the promptings of our maker. When God prompts us with a compelling insight from His Word, we should react with praise, for "More to be desired are they [His laws] than gold, yea, than much fine gold: sweeter also than honey and the honeycomb" (Ps. 19:10). When our God prompts us with a powerful confirmation of His presence, we should respond with joy, for as the psalmist wrote, "Thou wilt shew me the path of life: in thy presence is fulness of joy; at thy right hand there are pleasures for evermore" (Ps. 16:11). When our God prompts us with a terrifying reminder of His holiness, we should respond with fear, for it is written, "The fear of the LORD is the beginning of wisdom: and the knowledge of the holy is understanding" (Prov. 9:10). When God prompts us with a soothing touch of His grace, we should respond with love, for it is written, "We love him, because he first loved us" (1 John 4:19).

Prayer Intensified by the Majesty of God

Our seeker-sensitive generation, thinking in a commercial paradigm, is obsessed with treating worshipers as customers rather than as family members in a covenant relationship with God. This is why a pretentious familiarity and an inappropriately casual disposition are so often promoted. Reverential prayer is no longer considered necessary. The traditional expressions of respect, submission, and humility in prayer are considered optional or jettisoned, whether one is dealing with being suitably clothed for corporate worship, vocal tone, or body posture (kneeling, bowing the head, lifting the hands, closing the eyes, etc.).

One of the most striking elements of Abraham's prayer in Genesis 18 is that it initially appears to be overfamiliar with God. He seems to be talking to God as if they were equals. He is almost haggling with God in a way that seems inconsistent with the distinction between creature and creator. Abraham appears to be a man who will not take "yes" for an answer. Every time the Lord God agrees to grant him something, Abraham says, in effect, "That is not enough. I want some more." At first sight, such familiarity, aggressiveness, and assertiveness do not seem appropriate. For many devout believers, Abraham's prayer appears to lack the usual formality and respect one should use to address God. But appearances can be deceiving.

Even though Abraham's prayer may seem aggressive and familiar, a closer look reveals a deeper submission and humility that demonstrate that he had a firm grasp of God's majesty. Though Abraham was very persistent in his petitions to God, he was careful to make sure that he was understood and that it was clear that he knew his place. Just take a look at his deferential language in verse 27: "Behold now, I have taken upon me to speak unto the LORD, which am but dust and ashes." Verses 30–32 are similar: "Oh let not the LORD be angry, and I will speak." Abraham was appropriately scared. He knew he had entered a dangerous situation through this interaction with the Almighty, an encounter that could easily mean certain death.

This is a great paradox. Two seemingly contradictory attitudes are manifested in Abraham's prayer. On the one hand, Abraham was far more aware of his unworthiness and weakness than most worshipers are, especially those who approach God with no knowledge of the depth of their sin. Abraham was scared because he had a profound sense of his unworthiness before the majesty of God, knowing that he deserved nothing but the wrath of God. On the other hand, Abraham was at the same time far more confident that God is merciful and wants to bless us than many people are, especially those who approach God with no knowledge of the depth of His grace.

The paradox is that Abraham was both scared and confident simultaneously. His prayer was radical, for he was both cautious and risky in his petitions. He meticulously tested God's hand of holiness while passionately tugging at God's heart of love. The foundation for Abraham's fearful yet bold prayer was that he had a vision of God he did not invent. He was dealing with the true and living God, not a figment of his imagination and manipulation.

Human inventions of God generally gravitate to extremes. We either see God as exalted and remote or we see God as "gentle Jesus, meek and mild." We never design a god that is both infinitely holy and infinitely loving simultaneously. Abraham realized his God was real, present, powerful, and personal. He is the judge of all the earth, and His decisions are unchallengeable and irreproachable. He is both infinitely holy and infinitely loving. Because of this, Abraham's prayers could not be reduced to a mere formality. His prayers had to be intense and thoughtful in the light of God's majesty.

In the light of who God is, we should be careful of how we approach Him in prayer. Let there be no more vain and superstitious repetitions of particular words or phrases. We must abandon theatrical prayer presentations designed to impress the ignorant rather than to speak to our heavenly Father. We should, instead, begin to pay attention to the simplicity and profundity of the Lord's Prayer (Matt. 6:9–13), the model prayer, for we should give to the Lord in prayer precisely what He has required of us.

Prayer Influenced by the Mission of God

We live in narcissistic times—a reality often reflected in our prayers. Generally, our prayer interests are very narrow. There is usually a token offering of words of adoration, a brief and shallow confession of sin, and a few words of thanksgiving. Whereas petition and supplication comprise a significant portion of our prayer time.

Abraham's prayer in Genesis 18 is quite different. He gives us a powerful example of missional prayer. He does not pray for personal spiritual power, for strength for the day, or to get his needs met. His prayers were far more selfless than ours. Abraham leveraged his face-to-face relationship with God in order to intercede for the people of Sodom and Gomorrah. Despite their wickedness, he pleaded with the Lord on their behalf.

Sodom and Gomorrah were notoriously wicked cities: "And the LORD said, Because the cry of Sodom and Gomorrah is great, and because their sin is very grievous; I will go down now, and see whether they have done altogether according to the cry of it, which is come unto me; and if not, I will know" (Gen. 18:20–21). The Hebrew word translated *cry* (or *outcry*) often refers to the cries of the victims of violent injustice. When the Lord God spoke of the outcry, He referred to the oppression that poor and marginal people in Sodom and Gomorrah were experiencing. Of course, these cities were, and continue to be, synonymous with a sexual perversion of the worst kind, especially homosexuality. Still, they had other egregious transgressions that also motivated divine intervention and judgment (see Ezek. 16:49–50).

Abraham knew precisely how wicked those cities were, but he still begged the Lord to show them mercy: "And Abraham drew near, and said, Wilt thou also destroy the righteous with the wicked? Peradventure there be fifty righteous within the city: wilt thou also destroy and not spare the place for the fifty righteous that are therein?'" (Gen. 18:23–24). The word *spare* here means *forgive*. This shows that Abraham's concern was not simply to save his nephew, Lot, and his family who were living in Sodom. Indeed, Abraham never even mentions Lot. Rather, he was concerned about the pagan population of both cities. Though they were wicked and terrible cities, Abraham begged the Lord to spare them. He took his life into his hands to urge God to bless, forgive, and pardon Sodom and Gomorrah.

Abraham did not have a long list of personal petitions to lay before God. God had already reiterated his promise to provide a son for Abraham and Sarah (Gen. 18:10). Instead, Abraham poured himself out in prayer for the good of the people around him, including those doing the most egregious evil. He loved them despite their wickedness and cared about the people of these cities despite their iniquity. He focused his prayers on their spiritual needs, not their desires and wants. This is how we should be praying as well. Our prayers should be dominated by the needs of our community, especially the people in it whom we do not like and who surely do not like us.

In reality, it is far easier for us to hate the people who hate us, instead of pouring our hearts out in prayer on their behalf. Of course, there is nothing special about such a response. This is why the Lord Jesus Christ challenged His disciples, "But I say unto you, Love your enemies, bless them that curse you, do good to them that hate you, and pray for them which despitefully use you, and persecute you" (Matt. 5:44). Similarly, our Lord explained in verses 46 and 47 of the same chapter, "For if ye love them which love you, what reward have ye? do not even the publicans the same? And if ye salute your brethren only, what do ye more than others? do not even the publicans so?"

There is nothing special about exchanging blessings for blessings—that is simply a quid pro quo. But we set ourselves apart from the crowd when we can exchange blessings for cursing, good for evil, love for hate, courtesy for coldness, and tenderness for torture. We reflect God's character when we can sincerely pray even for those who oppose us, for those who are notoriously wicked. Abraham understood this well, for he spoke to God of mercy when righteous indignation could easily have kicked in. He risked his life to rescue the perishing when he could have played it safe and kept silent. Instead of using his access to God's power to serve his own personal interests, his words were fueled by compassion for those in need.

Prayer Informed by the Magnanimity of God

The radical nature of Abraham's prayer was grounded in his profound grasp of theological truth. As a result, Abraham's prayer proved to be a sophisticated interaction with God. His reasoning was focused on the attributes of God and flowed from an understanding of God's nature. For example, Abraham asked, "Shall not the Judge of all the earth do right?" (Gen. 18:25). This rhetorical question is practically a statement—of course God is a just God. Divine justice, dispensed in the ultimate tribunal of the universe, is unimpeachable. Abraham wanted to get a reprieve for Sodom and Gomorrah, but he knew that God was not going to abandon His holy justice.

Having affirmed the justice of God, Abraham had to find the connection between this justice and the concept of hope. God's justice is a vital attribute in this broken world we inhabit. When we look at the perpetual injustice of the world around us, there is no hope for the world unless there is a God of justice who is going to put everything right someday. Issues of theodicy—explaining what God is up to in this fallen world—cannot be divorced from His plan of redemption and restoration. Abraham's theological argument needed balance.

Abraham knew firsthand the magnanimous grace of God. In verses 17–19, God said, "Shall I hide from Abraham that thing which I do; seeing that Abraham shall surely become a great and mighty nation, and all the nations of the earth shall be blessed in him? For I know him, that he will command his children and his household after him, and they shall keep the way of the LORD, to do justice and judgment; that the LORD may bring upon Abraham that which he hath spoken of him." Abraham probably did not know the reasons why he had been chosen and called by God, but he knew that he had not been selected because he was perfect. He was aware of his sin and the many times he had failed the Lord. He had no delusions concerning his tarnished record and the corruptions of his own heart. But despite all his failures, Abraham marveled at the magnanimity of God's grace, mercy, love, and forbearance. Despite his sins of omission and his blatant transgressions, he noticed God was still willing to meet with him face-to-face. Abraham held on to the doctrine that God is a sparing God, a forgiving God, and a pardoning God—a God of free and sovereign grace.

Having reaffirmed the justice of God, Abraham balanced this with the love of God—a love that would even spare the undeserving. Thus, in verse 24, he asks an amazing question: O Lord, will you not spare these wicked cities for the sake of the righteous living among them? Abraham did not ask the Lord to lay aside His righteousness. That would be impossible. Instead, Abraham focused on God's infinite love for righteousness. He reasoned that perhaps the Lord could, in pursuit of the salvation of a righteous minority, allow some of the unrighteous in the vicinity to feast on the crumbs that fell from the table prepared for the elect. This was the same argument made in the New Testament by the Syrophenician woman, who asked the Lord Jesus to heal her demon-possessed daughter (Mark 7:25–26). Our Lord tested her faith by questioning her credentials to make such a request—as a gentile, surely her place was with dogs in the shadows, not with the family gathered around the table. She eloquently appealed to the Lord with the words, "Yes, Lord: yet the dogs under the table eat of the children's crumbs" (7:28).

Abraham's argument is fascinating. He knew that sometimes the guilt of the few is imputed to the many, a truth repeatedly demonstrated throughout the Old Testament. The sin of Achan and his family affected the whole camp of Israel at Jericho (see Joshua 7). David's sin concerning the rebellious census that he took resulted in the death of seventy thousand people (2 Samuel 24). Indeed, the sin of our first parents in the great fall plunged their entire posterity onto the trajectory to perdition, facing the full cup of God's wrath.

Yet here Abraham turned the question in the opposite direction. He asked, in effect, "Lord, would You consider allowing the righteousness of the few to be imputed to the many? Is it possible that, despite the bad record and wicked hearts in these cities, you would love the righteous minority so much that, for their sakes, you would forgive the undeserving, pagan residents?"

Abraham's approach was to honor the righteousness of God in a manner that would rescue the undeserving. Thus, repeatedly, Abraham begs for the same transaction, even though he is rapidly running out of righteous residents. Every time God says, "Yes," Abraham raises the stakes saying, in effect, "You would forgive the undeserving of these cities for this number of righteous folks. Lord, I do not want to sound ungrateful, for You have been most generous, but could we reduce the number of the righteous?" Abraham kept repeating this routine time after time, stunned by the magnanimity of God.

It went from fifty to forty-five to forty to thirty to twenty to ten. Abraham was successful in each petition, tugging at the heart of God's marvelous, infinite, matchless, and magnanimous grace. Then, quite suddenly, Abraham gave up asking. Why did he not ask about whether grace could cover the wicked for the sake of five righteous persons, or even one righteous person in the city? The answer is that Abraham knew these cities did not have a single resident who was infinitely righteous. Even those counted as righteous among men, like his nephew Lot (see 2 Peter 2:7), are always marked by some measure of corruption. No one possesses infinite righteousness. Infinite righteousness was required to save the cities, a righteousness that could not be found within Sodom or Gomorrah. Abraham understood the problem: an infinite debt needed an infinite payment. But he was stumped as to the solution: Who is that infinite One who could make a sufficient payment?

The good news is that, many centuries later, someone arrived who was qualified to complete what Abraham had started—Jesus of Nazareth. Abraham acted as an advocate, praying for Sodom and Gomorrah, the undeserving cities. He stood in front of God on behalf of the people, and he made intercession for them, but he could not succeed in rescuing them from the judgment to come. Abraham *risked* his life by going before God to save the people of Sodom and Gomorrah, but the Lord Jesus Christ came and *gave* His life to rescue the undeserving. Abraham said, in effect, "I am representing these people, Lord, but please do not be angry with me." Jesus Christ, however, represented us fully, taking the cosmic wrath of divine justice into His heart. His atonement on Calvary, that one act of pure, perfect love, was also an act of perfect righteousness that fully paid for our sins. When Jesus asked His Father, "Lord, will You save undeserving people for the sake of one righteous man?" God's answer was, "Yes! If that one is my only begotten Son, I am indeed well pleased to save all who are His—as many persons who demonstrate repentance and authentic saving faith, all those who truly believe" (see Heb. 7:25). God spares many who are undeserving for the sake of the One, the only begotten of the Father, full of grace and truth.

The truth is that we all have sinned far more egregiously than we would ever admit. There is dirt in the life of every child of Adam. Dirty thoughts, dirty desires, and dirty acts saturate our records and nature. We may not be listed as residents in Sodom and Gomorrah, but Sodom and Gomorrah are definitely resident in us. Yet the glorious gospel of Jesus Christ tells us that our God is far more gracious than we can imagine. By His grace and for His glory, Christ completed Abraham's incomplete prayer. The righteousness of the Lord Jesus Christ Himself can and will be imputed to all who can genuinely repent of their sins and place their faith in Him alone.

The gospel is not that good people are included and evil people are excluded. Rather, the gospel is that humble people who admit to their depravity are included, and the proud people who will never admit that they are evil are excluded. The gospel destroys the oppressive superiority that pretentious, moralistic people have. There is no point in boasting about sailing on a beautiful yacht of superiority when we are all in the same iniquitous boat. True conversion destroys our pride and gives us great compassion for all who share our frailty and tainted condition.

Do not be afraid to ask God for big things, even for things that might seem impossible. While we admire Abraham's persistence in prayer, we might be discouraged because he apparently did not get what he asked for. But Abraham did not leave empty-handed. His nephew, Lot, escaped with his children, even while his wife perished for looking back (Gen. 19:23–26). We are told in Genesis 19:29

that God rescued Lot and the children because Abraham had prayed this prayer: "And it came to pass, when God destroyed the cities of the plain, that God remembered Abraham, and sent Lot out of the midst of the overthrow, when he overthrew the cities in the which Lot dwelt." God always accomplishes His purpose in answering radical prayer.

Because God has all the power as well as all the love in the world for His children, we may approach our God with confidence: "Let us therefore come boldly unto the throne of grace, that we may obtain mercy, and find grace to help in time of need" (Heb. 4:16). Let us come boldly, not necessarily in a public, religious place, but to the throne of God's grace. Come boldly, not with a sense of entitlement, but in self-abasement. Come boldly, not with foolish decrees and declarations, but in contrition and confession. Come boldly, not because of who we are, but despite who we are and because of whose we are. To you, Christ boldly says, "Come unto me, all ye that labour and are heavy laden, and I will give you rest" (Matt. 11:28).

Chapter 5

RADICAL SUFFERING

Before we speak of radical suffering, some initial clarification is necessary. We are not celebrating masochism, as if we took some kind of pleasure in experiencing pain. Rather, our purpose is to demonstrate that the God of the Bible has a positive purpose in our lives for pain. If this is the case, then as true believers in Christ, we should not resent the presence of the pain that God actively permits; instead, we should embrace it. That is certainly easier said than done, but for the biblical Christian, it must be done.

Every one of us has experienced some measure of pain in our lives. Such pain sometimes seems to have no obvious cause, while at other times, the pain is being endured because of our own poor decisions. But there are also times when we suffer pain as a direct consequence of some of our wisest and most noble decisions. The latter continues to be a particular enigma to many people.

This notion of embracing our pain is hard to communicate in a culture filled with the voices of charismatic religious figures announcing that God is concerned only for our happiness. Moreover, many in our Western culture believe that it is not just the pursuit of happiness that is a fundamental right but happiness itself. Personal happiness is regarded as a basic human right that trumps other essential rights.

In such a context, we may notice that our Lord's treatment of suffering might be considered insensitive and politically incorrect in our generation. In Luke 13, Jesus commented on a recent tragedy at a place called Siloam where a tower had fallen, resulting in the deaths of eighteen people. The general assumption was that the victims must have been worse sinners than those around them, or such a terrible fate would never have befallen them. Today, a typical religious leader would offer bland platitudes, assuring the loved ones that the victims would be in their thoughts and prayers. Then they would quickly advise everyone that God could not possibly have had anything to do with the tragedy. Such leaders would be searching desperately for other possible objects of blame, but not God. In contrast, our Lord Jesus said, "I tell you, Nay: but, except ye repent, ye shall all likewise perish" (Luke 13:5). In effect, our Lord was saying, "No, of course, they were not worse sinners than you. You should be thrilled that no towers are falling on you right now—that is certainly what you deserve!"

Jesus's surprising response to this tragic event forces us to examine the unstated premises that lie behind our questions about suffering. Whenever someone asks, "Why does God allow all this evil and suffering in the world?" there is an assumption behind the question. The interrogator is convinced that God somehow owes us a comfortable, convenient, and trouble-free life. But the God of the Bible is not our servant, duty bound to do our bidding and satisfy our desires; He is the creator, sustainer, and upholder of our lives. Because of this, our moral obligation is to honor, serve, love, and obey Him with unrestrained and comprehensive joy, eager willingness, and unceasing reverence.

Unfortunately, we have done the exact opposite. We have all resented God's sovereignty and have characterized it as undue interference. We have rejected His loving authority over our lives. We have continually manifested the hubris of believing that we are wiser and know how to run the universe better than Him. We have resented God's moral and ethical precepts whenever they oppose our desires or what we thought was best. In all of this, God has been very patient with us. He has given us many chances to surrender ourselves to Him in worship and service, but we have repeatedly rebelled against His loving authority. In this context, we often dare to suggest that God owes us a comfortable life, as if we are the center of the universe and not He.

One of the purposes of 1 Peter is to explain to Peter's audience that Christians can face difficulties, troubles, and suffering and yet be transformed by those same events into far greater maturity and confidence. They (and we) should therefore embrace the arrival of pain in our lives, knowing that God is determined to use it for our sanctification. In the Christian life, suffering and glory are inextricably linked because our Savior, the Lord Jesus Christ, came into His glory through much grief. As 1 Peter 1:11 says, "Searching what, or what manner of time the Spirit of Christ which was in them did signify, when it testified beforehand the sufferings of Christ, and the glory that should follow." Our Lord's experience of suffering not only served to atone for our sins but also acts as a pattern for all of us.

In this respect, biblical Christianity has a quite different approach to suffering from many other religions and philosophies. Eastern religions generally look at suffering as an illusion that may be transcended. Meanwhile, Western secular culture typically looks at suffering as an absolute, unmitigated curse. In contrast, while biblical Christianity affirms the reality of suffering as an inevitable part of living in a fallen and cursed world, it also maintains an optimism about the good fruit that suffering may bear in our lives, which is quite different from the pessimism of the secular culture.

The reason that suffering and glory are inextricably linked in biblical Christianity is that in Christ we meet the one and only God-man, who Himself triumphed through suffering. The biblical God is the only God who has experienced pain and who can therefore speak sympathetically to our pain. It is written in Hebrews 4:15, "For we have not an high priest which cannot be touched with the feeling of our infirmities; but was in all points tempted like as we are, yet without sin." In our experience of pain we gain some semblance of appreciation of the pain that Christ Himself suffered. At the same time, it is the far greater pain that He suffered for us that gives meaning to our pain and facilitates our sanctification.

The suffering of true disciples of Christ after the pattern of their Savior is profoundly real; it is not an illusion. Our intimacy with God grows because of the mutuality and solidarity of the Creator and the creature in the experience of suffering. This was why David could look at God and call Him, "My God," something that would be unthinkable in Islam. A devout Muslim would never refer to the Allah of the Koran as, "My Allah." False religion knows nothing of a worshiper receiving that level of intimacy with their god. Even with the infinite disparity of being between God and us, the inextricable link between suffering and glory in our God amazingly finds a finite replication in the life of the true disciple of Christ. We, too, powerfully experience the link between suffering and glory.

The Vital Importance of Doctrine

While the whole first chapter of 1 Peter addresses these issues with great profundity, one verse in particular captures the matter of the necessity of Christian disciples embracing the sufferings and griefs that come with following Christ. It is 1 Peter 1:6, where Peter encourages his hearers to endure suffering in the light of the great salvation they have received, "Wherein ye greatly rejoice, though now for a season, if need be, ye are in heaviness through manifold temptations."

The context leading up to this verse is of great importance. In the first five verses of 1 Peter, the apostle Peter gives us the order of salvation. He begins with the fact that we are foreknown or, we might say, "foreloved" by God. God set His love on us and chose us in Christ in eternity past (1 Peter 1:2; Eph. 1:4). In the course of time, He sent the Spirit to sanctify us, to set us apart as His holy people, which results in the new birth that brings us to faith in Christ (1 Peter 1:2). How are we born again? Well, our Lord Jesus died on the cross and rose from the dead (1:3). Then, the Holy Spirit applies that gospel to our hearts so that we believe. Christ's blood is sprinkled on our souls, and we are forgiven of all our sins (1:2). But that is not all. We then grow in grace and sanctification, gradually becoming more and more holy (1:4). Throughout this process, God is holding on to us, shielding us, keeping us by His power until the last moment of history in which suddenly God will appear in order to vindicate His people (1:5). The glory of God comes down into our lives, and we receive our full inheritance, which is the joy of being made perfect and being with God forever (1:4). Hallelujah!

First Peter 1:1–5 thus gives us a brief summary of the theology of the Christian life—foreknowledge leads to sovereign election, election leads to divine calling, and calling leads to regeneration. That then leads to repentance and faith and the sprinkling of the blood, which in turn leads to sanctification. Sanctification leads to obedience, and that leads, finally, to glorification on the last day.

The point of this condensed theology is joy. Peter says, "Wherein ye greatly rejoice" (1 Peter 1:6). The apostle Peter teaches us that if we know this profound doctrine, we can maintain a sense of joy amid our deepest grief and pain. We are not rejoicing because we have been to therapy, or because we have found emotional release, or because our suffering and pain is not real. Far from it. We are rejoicing because we know the truth about God and about ourselves.

As a pastor for nearly four decades, I have been at the bedside of many souls when they are dying. When believers are dying, they do not want to hear that God has nothing to do with their pain. Rather, they need a preacher to tell them about the refiner's fire and that God is burning off the dross so that there is pure gold in the end (Mal. 3:3). They need someone bold enough to say, "For me to live is Christ, and to die is gain" (Phil. 1:21). They need someone with the courage to announce, "For whether we live, we live unto the Lord; and whether we die, we die unto the Lord: whether we live therefore, or die, we are the Lord's" (Rom. 14:8).

Many people turn their noses up at the idea of doctrine. They are convinced that doctrinal talk is the cause of a lot of the fighting and acrimony in the Christian world. They shout, "We want love, not doctrine!" Yet the apostle Peter makes the case that it is precisely a grasp of profound doctrine that will get us through the pain and suffering that is inevitable in this world. Theological and biblical ignorance will only serve to exacerbate our problems by giving us false expectations about God and life that make us bitter and cynical, and ultimately lead us to despair. We must certainly acknowledge that Christianity is far more than doctrine. This will be obvious when we look at the rest of verse 6. But biblical Christianity is never less than doctrine.

When our backs are against the wall, we need the Rock of ages, not shifting sand. When the foundations of our lives are shaken, we need solid doctrine above all else. We will never deal adequately with our suffering unless we can set it in the context of the great salvation we have received in Christ. Only as we rejoice in these beautiful truths will we be equipped against the assaults of the Evil One and the lies of our culture, so that we may stand firm in the face of the worst this world has to offer.

The Vital Importance of Suffering

The pain that God has permitted in our lives is not without purpose. The second phrase of 1 Peter 1:6 says, "though now for a season, if need be." In other words, "though now for a little while, if necessary." The apostle Peter declares here that if grief or troubles come into our lives right now, it is because we need the affliction, even if it is excruciating. Our God has lovingly and purposely permitted the pain, and so it must be essential to our spiritual health. According to John Newton, "All shall work together for good: everything is needful that He sends; nothing can be needful that He withholds."[1] Equally, if pain is *not* in our lives, then we do not need it—even though we may think we do. God knows what He is doing. He may be letting the pain into our lives in stages and in ways that will teach us the things He wants us to learn that we would not learn in any other way.

This understanding of God's purposes through pain might not resonate with someone whose life seems chaotic and out of control right now. It may be hard for us to discern the ordering of our lives because it is not *our* order. It is God's order, agenda, and schedule, so it should not surprise us that it appears chaotic to us. But there is

---

1. John Newton, *The Works of John Newton* (London: Hamilton, Adams, and Co., 1824; Edinburgh: Banner of Truth, 1985), 2:147.

order even if we cannot discern God's plan. We must trust our God that there is order and meaning, as well as a trajectory to ultimate glory in whatever pain God has ordained for our lives.

We will never learn who we are without suffering. Suffering shows us our faults and our flaws. It confronts us with ourselves in a way that nothing else does—it exposes our lack of patience, our lack of foresight, our addictions, our foolishness, our ego, our immorality, our failures, and so on. Discovering the truth about oneself is an essential gift from God, even if it comes wrapped in much pain. There is no other way to deliver this package.

Peter also reminds us that suffering is temporary: it is only for a little while, "for a season" (1 Peter 1:6). There will be an end to it. The pain comes to us according to God's timing, and it will leave according to the same schedule, when it has done its work. When we are suffering, we may need to repeat to ourselves often in disciplined moments of meditation, "This is not my schedule; it is God's schedule."

We must also remember that the God who brings this suffering into our lives is our Father. It was our heavenly Father who appointed these things to facilitate our growth. His goal in all of this is articulated by the apostle Paul: "That I may know him, and the power of his resurrection, and the fellowship of his sufferings, being made conformable unto his death" (Phil. 3:10). As Paul embraced the pain and suffering that his heavenly Father brought into his life, it did not oppress him or immobilize him—rather, it motivated and energized him.

We should learn to celebrate the fact that our God does not always give us what we want. Some of the best answers to our prayers begin with, "No," or "Wait." We should be grateful that our God wisely and lovingly gives us what we need. This requires profound faith, for we must trust the One who sees the end from the beginning. We are always tempted to take the path of least resistance, and we cry out for immediate relief. However, by faith, we must embrace the truth "that the sufferings of this present time are not worthy to be compared with the glory which shall be revealed in us" (Rom. 8:18). As the apostle

Paul wrote, "And he said unto me, My grace is sufficient for thee: for my strength is made perfect in weakness. Most gladly therefore will I rather glory in my infirmities, that the power of Christ may rest upon me" (2 Cor. 12:9). Or as the psalmist reminds us, "Weeping may endure for a night, but joy cometh in the morning" (Ps. 30:5). Indeed, "Our light affliction, which is but for a moment, worketh for us a far more exceeding and eternal weight of glory" (2 Cor. 4:17).

Living with Balance

Immaturity gravitates toward oversimplification, thinking that you must be either happy or you are sad. But the Christian life is far more nuanced. Those who endure pain come to accept that both extremes of emotional experience must be lived out with some semblance of balance. The last phrase of 1 Peter 1:6 reads, "ye are in heaviness through manifold temptations." In other words, it is perfectly normal to be distressed or grieved by trials and temptations.

In our text, *grieved* (or *heaviness*) refers to being deeply troubled. This conjures up an image of stormy seas. In Antigua and Barbuda, we have some of the best beaches in the world. But after a hurricane, our beautiful, transparent, turquoise water looks like a filthy, muddy swamp. The turmoil and tumult of the storm has stirred everything up into an ugly mess. In the same way, our pain and suffering can stir up our hearts and bring into the open all kinds of messy emotions. We have the joy that comes from the gospel, but we also struggle with fear, anger, and frustration.

Christians should not be surprised when this happens. Peter describes people who are rejoicing, but they are also grieving. Both emotions are present at the same time. The text does not say that they are rejoicing now though they *were* troubled, and it does not say that they are *not* rejoicing now because they *are* troubled. It says they are rejoicing now, and they are also deeply troubled. The Bible repeatedly shows that Christians do not just experience pain, suffering, and grief; they are affected by it.

The Christian faith allows us to be radically honest about our feelings. The apostle Paul wrote in 2 Corinthians 4:8–9, "We are troubled on every side, yet not distressed; we are perplexed, but not in despair; persecuted, but not forsaken; cast down, but not destroyed." That is precisely what the apostle Peter is talking about in our text. Because of the gospel, biblical Christians may be both very troubled and happy simultaneously. Indeed, experiencing profound emotions is a normal characteristic of someone deeply affected by the gospel. Genuine Christians are often deeply troubled. Even our Lord Jesus, the epitome of perfect joy, actually wept at the graveside of Lazarus (John 11:35). The more perfect you are, the more holy you are, the more you will be deeply troubled by the brokenness and pain around you.

When the gospel gets into our hearts and we see that we are utterly loved and fully accepted by the same God we have so deeply offended, we have the emotional freedom to admit the many sins in our lives. Until we reach that point, we are far more likely to live in denial. It takes genuine regeneration to enable us to admit with the apostle Paul, "For I know that in me (that is, in my flesh,) dwelleth no good thing: for to will is present with me; but how to perform that which is good I find not" (Rom. 7:18). We now gladly admit with the same apostle, "Unto me, who am less than the least of all saints, is this grace given, that I should preach among the Gentiles the unsearchable riches of Christ" (Eph. 3:8).

Apart from the gospel of Jesus Christ, it is hard for people to admit how wicked they are because they have no solution for their sin. As a result, they make excuses for it. They say, "Well, yes, I know it's not right, but nobody's perfect." But when the gospel penetrates deep into our hearts, we finally have enough hope to admit how bad things are. We feel the hurt of other people whose plight we share, and we are free to come alongside them as fellow sinners and fellow sufferers.

Christians do not merely *experience* suffering, they are deeply *affected* by it—not just their own, but the sufferings of others as well. They sense the troubles of the world more than ever before. Christianity is quite different from a stoic denial of the reality of our pain. At the same time, Christians also have a sublime hope, a hope to which Peter refers in 1 Peter 1:8: "Whom having not seen, ye love;

in whom, though now ye see him not, yet believing, ye rejoice with joy unspeakable and full of glory."

Problems appear when this equilibrium between suffering and hope is lost in our lives and our grief overwhelms our hope. While Christian hope will ultimately overcome our grief, it does not immediately eradicate it. Rather, it provides a counterweight that balances grief, driving us to draw deeply from our resources in Christ and the gospel.

Our hope of "joy unspeakable and full of glory" enables us to say, "Thank You," to God for both the smiling and the frowning providences. It reminds us that He does all things in this world well. This hope will silence all the murmuring, self-pity, complaining, and covetousness in our lives. With August L. Storm, we may sing unto the Lord:

> Thanks for roses by the wayside,
> Thanks for thorns their stems contain!
> Thanks for home and thanks for fireside,
> Thanks for hope, that sweet refrain!
> Thanks for joy and thanks for sorrow,
> Thanks for heav'nly peace with Thee!
> Thanks for hope in the tomorrow,
> Thanks through all eternity![2]

Our God Himself is our ultimate resource in effectively facing pain. The Puritan, George Swinnock, once wrote,

> If the world's darlings enjoy many good things, they lack all without Christ. God is all good things, and every good thing. He is self-sufficient, alone-sufficient, and all-sufficient. If God were your portion, you would find in Him whatsoever your heart could desire, and tend to your happiness. Are you ambitious? He is a crown of glory. Are you covetous? He is unsearchable riches and righteousness. Do you desire pleasure? He is rivers of pleasures and fullness of joy. Are you hungry? He is a feast of wine on the lees and the fat things full of marrow. Are you

---

2. August L. Storm, "Thanks to God for My Redeemer," 1891; trans. Carl. E. Backstrom, 1931.

weary? He is rest, a shadow from the heat, and a shelter from the storm. Are you weak? He is everlasting strength. Are you doubting? He is marvellous in counsel. Are you in darkness? He is the Sun of righteousness. Are you sick? He is the God of your health. Are you sorrowful? He is the God of all consolations. Whatever your calamity, He can remove it. Whatever your necessity, He can relieve it. He is silver, gold, honor, delight, food, raiment, house, land, peace, wisdom, power, beauty, father, mother, wife, husband, mercy, love, grace, glory, and infinitely more than all these. There are all sorts of delights in Him. He is the tree of life bearing all manner of fruits, and a variety of all comforts. See God, and you see all. Enjoy God, and enjoy all.[3]

---

3. George Swinnock, *The Works of George Swinnock, M.A.* (Edinburgh: James Nichol, 1868), 4:40. The quote has been slightly abridged and modernized.

Chapter 6

RADICAL RESISTANCE

Almost all nations that experience an influx of immigrants have concerns about assimilation. People from diverse backgrounds and belief systems undergo assimilation when they come to view themselves as part of the wider community. Whether you are talking about ideas, or nutrients, or immigration, *assimilation* describes the act of taking something in and absorbing it entirely. Culturally, assimilation is often welcomed by those who are in the dominant group, who desire to preserve their values and customs. Meanwhile, some minority groups resist it because they fear losing their identity and being absorbed into the dominant culture.

Yet assimilation can also take place in spiritual matters. In a culture where the church is rapidly losing its influence and there is sometimes open hostility to the Christian faith, some believers are seeking to accommodate the world in order to mitigate the acrimony and hostility they would otherwise experience. How, though, should we think biblically about such attempts to seek worldly accreditation and approbation?

The book of Daniel is particularly relevant to this question. At that time, in the early sixth century BC, Babylon was the preeminent power in the world. The Babylonians had a great empire and conquered people throughout much of the known world. Whenever they went in and defeated a land, they then exiled many people, especially the professional classes. This deportation included artisans, scholars, priests, and government officials, including the military officers and nobility. They took these exiles and forced them to live in Babylon, where they sought to assimilate them into Babylonian culture and customs. In this way, they removed potential rebels from their power base in their home country and hoped that they would eventually adopt the values and the standards of Babylon. As they lost their own distinctive culture, beliefs, and values, and Babylon became home, the hope was that they would stop resisting the claims of the empire.

The book of Daniel is a story primarily about Daniel, a Jewish exile, and his three friends, Shadrach, Meshach, and Abednego, and their confrontations in Babylon with its emperor, Nebuchadnezzar, as they refused to assimilate to his demands. How would they fare in their desire to remain true to the faith of their fathers in an alien and sometimes hostile environment?

Contempt for Exclusivity

By Daniel 3, Shadrach, Meshach, and Abednego (to give them their Babylonian names) had already been appointed to positions of power and influence, alongside Daniel, because of their evident wisdom and trustworthiness. They were successfully climbing the career ladder in their enforced new home. But then came a moment of truth: Nebuchadnezzar built a massive statue just outside Babylon, and he summoned representatives from all over the empire to come and bow down in worship to the statue he had set up (Dan. 3:1–5). And so everyone did as the king commanded—everyone, that is, except Shadrach, Meshach, and Abednego (3:6–12; Daniel must have arranged to be elsewhere that day).

When the attention of the Babylonian monarch, Nebuchadnezzar, was drawn to these three men still standing erect while everyone else prostrated themselves, he asked them, "Is it true, O Shadrach, Meshach, and Abednego, do not ye serve my gods, nor worship the golden image which I have set up?" (Dan. 3:14). Of course, Shadrach, Meshach, and Abednego would not do it, as men who were committed to honoring the true and living God. The punishment for disobedience was that offenders would be thrown into a blazing furnace.

Interestingly, the image Nebuchadnezzar set up is never given a name. The Babylonians had several gods, but we are not told that the name of any particular deity was attached to the statue. In fact, Nebuchadnezzar may provide a hint as to what the statue represented in his question to the Hebrews. Scholars tell us that a possible alternative translation of verse 14 would be, "Is it true, Shadrach, Meshach, and Abednego, that you do not serve my gods *by* worshipping the image of gold I have set up?" In this view, the image of gold does not represent one god; it represents *all* the gods, values, beliefs, and essentially the culture of Babylon.

Nebuchadnezzar knew that his capital was cosmopolitan and pluralistic. There were people from many lands, and they all had different religions and gods. He said to everyone, in effect, "I am not asking that you worship my gods (the Babylonian gods) *instead* of your god; I am asking that you worship the Babylonian gods in *addition* to your gods." He was making it abundantly clear that they had permission to worship whatever gods they chose. But the law was that they had to affirm the officially sanctioned religion and values publicly. In other words, to address the same principle with a twenty-first-century issue, we may say, "I am not asking you to abandon your view of biblical marriage; I am just requiring you to endorse and even participate in our redefinitions of other kinds of marriages—or you will be charged with hate crimes and a violation of civil rights."

Those who did not affirm the exclusivity of their god would have had few problems with Nebuchadnezzar's decree. They were happy to affirm pluralism and add yet one more deity to their pantheon. Alternatively, they could privatize their faith, worshiping their own god in private, but in public, adopting a pluralistic religion like everybody else. The same pressure to conform is applied in our wicked generation. We are told, "Privately, you can worship the way you want, but in public, you must bow to the demands of pluralism. You may not make exclusive claims for your religion." That is how most pluralistic societies work—they seek to assimilate you into the public culture by forcing you to privatize your faith.

Shadrach, Meshach, and Abednego would have none of it. These were not people who were hidden away in a tiny monastic enclave withdrawn from the world. Shadrach, Meshach, and Abednego, along with Daniel, were deeply involved in the culture of Babylon. They had received a Babylonian education. They were working in the public service as civil servants and were thus a part of the establishment. They were following the Lord's instruction to serve the city of Babylon, pray for it, work for its prosperity, and engage in the city's cultural and economic activities (see Jer. 29:7). But there was a line they could not cross—when asked to privatize their faith, these men said, "No! We cannot do that, no matter what the consequences are." That took real courage on their part.

The question for each of us here is, have we assimilated into the culture of our communities, schools, and workplaces, or are we resisting the pressure? If you do not understand the question, then you may already have assimilated and chosen pluralism, possibly without much thought or deliberation. You have agreed with the notion that everyone, no matter what he believes, should have his position treated with equal respect and should be granted equal credibility and dignity. You have embraced the cultural concept that no one's views may be rejected, for that would be bigotry. You have bowed to the value which states that "getting along" with one another is ultimately more important than the truth. The issues of ancient Babylon are not far from the issues of our own day.

Conflict of Interest

Nebuchadnezzar, the Babylonian king, was of course furious at what he perceived to be an act of treason by Shadrach, Meshach, and Abednego. These three Hebrew government members were publicly defying him to his face by not bowing down to the idol he set up. In Daniel 3:17–18, we read Shadrach, Meshach, and Abednego's response to the king's renewed ultimatum of *bow down or die* (vv. 14–15). They said to Nebuchadnezzar, "If it be so, our God whom we serve is able to deliver us from the burning fiery furnace, and he will deliver us out of thine hand, O king. But if not, be it known unto thee, O king, that we will not serve thy gods, nor worship the golden image which thou hast set up."

This is a truly remarkable declaration. Look at the first part of that statement. They essentially said, "We believe that our God is able to save us. He can certainly rescue us from your hand." They did not just say that God *can*; they said, in effect, "We believe that God *will*. We are convinced that God wants to. But even if He does not, we will still not bow down to that image." These were men of profound principle. But even principles can disappear or melt with the right amount of pressure. Something deeper is required.

These men maintained their principles in the face of the greatest pressure because they had no conflict of interest—they were focused exclusively on the glory of God. They were not demanding that God serve their interests; they understood that it was their duty to bow to God's interests alone. They made it abundantly clear to Nebuchadnezzar that their love for God was unconditional. They were not involved with their God to get anything, whether it was protection, material comfort, social standing, or personal fame. They were ready to give their God anything, even sacrificially.

Some of us may be very disappointed in God right now. We may not be prepared to admit it publicly, but it may still be true. Some may be ready to abandon the ministry, or even the church, and embrace the broader culture of worldliness. Such people may feel that they have followed the rules and led a pretty good life, yet there are a few things in this life that they have asked for and been denied. They want to know why they are expected to keep trusting in God and giving their all to Him while not getting what they want in return.

If that is our attitude, it has to be asked whether we are serving God at all, or if our efforts have simply been an attempt to use God. Our lives have never really been about God; what we were really invested in was our own agenda. We thought, "If I obey God, and I pray to God, God will give me what I want." But if I do not get what I want, there is no reason to hang around and keep on serving.

This was not the position of these three Hebrew young men. They were prepared to trust God, whatever the cost. They had no hidden agenda. For them, God was to be obeyed because He is God, not because they would get something in return. So, too, we should trust God, love Him, and serve Him because of who He is, not for what we hope to get out of it. Our purpose is to serve the divine agenda, not further our own agenda. This is a question that each of us needs to settle in our own lives. Do we believe that our God is enough for us? Is He able to deliver us according to His Word? And if He does not, are we willing to lay down our very lives for Him?

These young Hebrews had concluded that if God chose not to rescue them *from* death, then He would still rescue them *through* death. Whatever Nebuchadnezzar did to them, they had already won. If you die in the right relationship with God, you will wake up in His arms. There will be nothing but freedom, liberation, and joy. As a result, Christians are always safe, in life or in death. Our God is worthy of whatever sacrifices He calls us to make, because He is altogether lovely, the fairest of ten thousand, the bright and morning star.

Confusion about Affliction

Nebuchadnezzar was livid. His indignation was set ablaze by the blatant treason of Shadrach, Meshach, and Abednego. He had his servants heat the fire in the furnace seven times hotter than it already was (Dan. 3:19). Then he had Shadrach, Meshach, and Abednego bound and thrown into it. The narrative makes it clear that the furnace was so hot that the soldiers who threw them in died because of the heat (v. 22).

Then Nebuchadnezzar positioned himself at some vantage point where he could look into the furnace. He was stunned by two things that he saw. The first thing he saw was that these three men were walking around in the furnace (v. 25). Remember, his soldiers had died from just getting near the furnace, and these three rebels were inside the furnace walking around! The second, even more shocking, thing was that there were not just three men in the furnace; a fourth man had somehow joined them. Who was he? Nebuchadnezzar was at a loss for words, and said to his counselors, "Did not we cast three men bound into the midst of the fire? They answered and said unto the king, True, O king. He answered and said, Lo, I see four men loose, walking in the midst of the fire, and they have no hurt; and the form of the fourth is like the Son of God" (vv. 24–25). The three Hebrew men had been rescued by their God after all.

This amazing story teaches us some important lessons about suffering. First, we live in a sinful world, so we should not be surprised by suffering. Ever since man first sinned, suffering has become the new norm. The corruption that sin brought to our world is not merely cosmetic—it went to the core of everything. Job 5:7 says, "Yet man is born unto trouble, as the sparks fly upward." First Peter 4:12 is even more pointed, "Beloved, think it not strange concerning the fiery trial which is to try you, as though some strange thing happened unto you."

In my experience, it is often those who are relatively comfortable economically who are most likely to struggle with suffering. Almost everybody else (that is, most of the world) expects to suffer sooner or later, and sees it as inevitable. But those who do well financially are often blindsided by suffering. This is particularly true for people who live a relatively moral and upright life. They think their resources and their good life should protect them against painful realities.

The obvious answer to all this is that our Lord Jesus lived a perfect life, and yet His life was filled with suffering. This was not an accident, but the Lord's design for His servant (see Isa. 53:3). If that was God's plan for His beloved only Son, why should any of us be exempt? There are furnaces in life, and God's people should expect to have to walk through the fire (Isa. 43:2). Far too many Christians are deeply shaken by the experience of suffering because no one ever warned them to anticipate it. This is not right.

The second lesson we may learn from Daniel 3 is that God uses our trials to bring about transformative change in our lives. God has established that suffering relates to character like fire relates to gold. We saw this truth already in 1 Peter 1:6–7, "Wherein ye greatly rejoice, though now for a season, if need be, ye are in heaviness through manifold temptations: that the trial of your faith, being much more precious than of gold that perisheth, though it be tried with fire, might be found unto praise and honour and glory at the appearing of Jesus Christ."

Our faith going through suffering is like gold going through the fire. What does fire do to gold? It makes it better, more beautiful, and purer. We will never become contented people who are fully satisfied in Christ until suffering forces us to come to the end of ourselves and see that we deserve nothing because of our sin. We will never become sympathetic people with hearts of compassion until suffering forces us to experience something of the horrors and the pains that others experience when they suffer. Suffering humbles us by revealing our hearts and showing how easily we may grumble and complain against God, as well as fall into various temptations. We actually need suffering.

The reality is that there is no way to know who we are until we are tested. There is no way to learn how to trust in God until we are drowning in desperation. There is no way to empathize with other suffering people unless we have suffered. If we hold on to Jesus as we go through it, our suffering will actually refine our character as fire refines pure gold.

There is one more critical lesson about suffering that we must learn from Daniel 3. Many people are destroyed by suffering, instead of being refined by it. Suffering sometimes leads people to abandon their faith or to slide off the upright path. What do we have to know in order to grow and be purified by our suffering instead of being destroyed by it? The answer is that we need to know that we have an intermediary between God and us, someone standing in solidarity with us in the fires of our lives. We cannot make it through the furnace on our own.

In Daniel 3, we learn that one "like the Son of God" (or one like a son of the gods) appeared to minister to these three men of God amid the fiery furnace (v. 25). Nebuchadnezzar thought this was God's angel, sent to protect Shadrach, Meshach, and Abednego (v. 28). But this was no mere angel; it was nothing less than God in a visible form, a preincarnate manifestation of our Lord Jesus Christ Himself. Centuries earlier God had promised his people, "Fear not: for I have redeemed thee, I have called thee by thy name; thou art mine. When thou passest through the waters, I will be with thee; and through the rivers, they shall not overflow thee: when thou walkest through the fire, thou shalt not be burned; neither shall the flame kindle upon thee. For I am the LORD thy God, the Holy One of Israel, thy Saviour" (Isa. 43:1–3). He made good on that promise, as Christ entered the furnace to be with those three young men.

Yet entering the Babylonian furnace was a mere dress rehearsal for the day Jesus would endure the ultimate furnace for us on the cross of Calvary. His suffering there for us removes the sting of our suffering and enables us to know His presence with us in the midst of our deepest pains. When we understand Christ's mediation for us at the cross, accomplishing the forgiveness of all our sins and making us right with God, then all the other furnaces in our lives will be cut down to size and they will intimidate us no more. The hymn writer, Ethelyn Robinson Taylor, puts it like this:

> Far dearer than all
> That the world can impart
> Was the message that came to my heart.
> How that Jesus alone
> For my sin did atone,
> And Calvary covers it all.
>
> Calvary covers it all,
> My past with its sin and stain;
> My guilt and despair
> Jesus took on Him there,
> And Calvary covers it all.[1]

The cross of Calvary is not like the insurance policies of this world, where we have to read the fine print to ensure that every risk is properly covered. This is not the case when we are covered by the

---

1. Ethelyn Robinson Taylor, "Calvary Covers It All," 1934.

blood of Jesus—that crimson tide that washes us white as snow. Our guilt, shame, filth, and self-righteousness are all covered, and our fellowship with our heavenly Father is fully restored. When we know that, our time in the furnace will transform our dross into pure gold.

Chapter 7

RADICAL MISSIONS

Over the years, there have been a variety of wet blankets thrown over the evangelistic and missionary enterprises of the church. These are designed to discourage the cause of gospel outreach and dampen our zeal for the extension of the kingdom of God. They seek to eclipse the glorious zeal for lost souls that characterized the biblical and evangelical Calvinism that motivated past generations. Fueled by their confidence in the sovereignty of God over all things, including salvation, Reformed Christians drove the modern missions movement.

Mission-minded churches support the proclamation of the person and work of Jesus Christ to every place, tongue, tribe, people, and nation, near or far. To proclaim Jesus Christ is to declare that He is God Himself come down to earth and that He is the answer to the meaning of history and every life. This emphasis on the mission of God in Jesus to save people is radically different from virtually all other religions. Other religions seek to aid people in reaching up to a god, who, for the most part, is generally hidden and aloof. In contrast, biblical Christianity presents Jesus Christ as the true and living God who has come down to man.

Some are opposed to Christian mission because they think it constitutes imperialism. The charge is that Christian missionaries go to places where people already have their own religion and traditions, and they impose a culturally alien religion in Christianity. It is suggested that we should instead respect the religious practices of other cultures and not seek to impose foreign values on them by proselytizing them with a narrow Christian worldview.

Of course, those who are biblically and confessionally grounded cannot accept such claims, which entirely bypass the question of truth. Such ideas flow from a conviction that all religions are equally valid, a conviction that is entirely at odds with biblical Christianity's claim to possess exclusive truth. No discussion of missions can avoid this matter. Is Jesus *the* way or merely *a* way? It makes a world of difference whether we sing, "On Christ the solid rock I stand, all other ground is sinking sand,"[1] or, "On Christ the solid rock I stand; other rocks are available." Most people will allow us to say that we stand on Christ alone; what gets us into trouble is the part about "all other ground is sinking sand."

The Lord Jesus Himself pointed out the exclusivity of His mission when He said, "No man knoweth the Son, but the Father; neither knoweth any man the Father, save the Son" (Matt. 11:27). This may appear to be an inconsequential statement for many, but it makes the extraordinary claim that only the Father—only God—can know Jesus, for He is infinite, and only through Jesus can anyone come to know the true and living God. This audacious statement is the height of arrogance and intolerance—unless, of course, what Jesus says is absolutely true.

The World's Intolerance

One of the ongoing problems of Christian missions is that it has been, and always will be, misunderstood and slandered. In our generation, the primary challenge is to fight the charge of intolerance. We must fight this charge, for we know that the opposite is true.

The earlier verses provide the context for Jesus's claim. Matthew 11:25 reads, "At that time Jesus answered and said, I thank thee, O Father, Lord of heaven and earth, because thou hast hid these things from the wise and prudent, and hast revealed them unto babes." Over the years, many people have misunderstood this as saying that relatively few educated people will be believers (the wise and the learned) and that, for the most part, only uneducated people will

---

1. Edward Mote, "My Hope is Built on Nothing Less," 1834.

believe in Christianity. That is *not* what our Lord Jesus is saying here. Rather, our Lord's point is simple: the arrogant are content to continue a futile search while the humble are willing to ask for directions. The pretentious intelligentsia of every generation cling to their hypothetical and dramatic speculations about reality on their unending quest for truth. At the same time, humble people are open to listen to the only consistent explanation of reality known to man, which is biblical Christianity.

There are two approaches here. The Lord Jesus exposes those who would call Him arrogant, even while they themselves insist that divine revelation is not worthy of intelligent consideration. They look down on His biblical claims and, without thinking, assume that such claims have nothing to offer. So, their vain speculation continues with no end in sight. Many intellectuals are blatantly anti-intellectual, for they are closed to even looking at the biblical claims of Christ. They attempt to probe questions like the meaning of life, the problem of evil, the existence of God, and the essence of morality, while ignoring a whole body of theological knowledge given to us by God.

Our Lord makes a sharp distinction between those on this pretentious journey and those he calls "babes." The babes are humble people who refuse to let intellectual prejudice eliminate credible options. These are the people whose only agenda is to find the truth, the people whose only allegiance is to the evidence and to that which is logically consistent. These people not only consider the claims of those looking up to find God but also consider the claims of the one who came down from God—the incarnate God, Jesus Himself. These people are content to let all voices present their case, even the audacious voice of Christ with His exclusive claims.

Our Lord made it abundantly clear that if you are sure that there are no specific or definitive answers, which is the position of many in our postmodern generation, you will get none. God generally withholds the light from those who are confident in their darkness. If you rule out the possibility of revelation, you will never encounter God's truth. You cannot see if your eyes are shut; something must open your eyes if you are to discern the truth of God. Those who claim to be wise and prudent may also claim to be tolerant and inclusive, but they are the exact opposite. Who is shutting the doors of inquiry? It is not the babes in this text. They are humble enough to consider divine revelation. They will say, "If God has indeed come down, let us hear what He has to say." That is true tolerance and inclusivity.

The apostle Paul similarly condemns the claimed wisdom of this world in 1 Corinthians 1:20, where he says, "Where is the wise? where is the scribe? where is the disputer of this world? hath not God made foolish the wisdom of this world?" By trying to reach up to God with man-made religion (or its secular equivalent), humanity has not known God. God has shown that human wisdom is utter foolishness. Worldly wisdom resents any claim to exclusive truth. So, when our Lord declares, "I am the way, the truth, and the life: no man cometh unto the Father, but by me" (John 14:6), the world calls it narrow-minded bigotry. Yet there is a logical problem with this position. Anyone who dismisses an exclusive truth statement as being intrinsically invalid can only do so by making another claim to possess exclusive truth themself. It is an absurd, contradictory, and self-defeating position.

The wisdom of this world is inherently foolish. Sin makes us stupid and very proud of it. To say that nobody has all the truth may sound very inclusive, but such a statement is in itself a claim of superior truth. In the same way, those who argue that proselytizing is imperialistic and wrong are themselves proselytizing and insisting that others adopt their view. If those who are against Christian missions are trying to show us that we are wrong in our theological understanding, why should we be denied the opportunity to show others that their view of reality is wrong?

The truth is that no one can avoid exclusivity. Ultimately, everybody comes to some beliefs that they think are universally true. Abusing children is wrong, sex trafficking is wrong, Hitler's killing of six million Jews was wrong—few people are willing to abandon all absolutes. But even if they abandon all other absolutes, they must hold on to one affirmation: that Jesus Christ was *not* the infinite God-man who came to save us from our sins. Relativism is a self-defeating position. Those who affirm it are telling other people not to do the very thing they are doing whenever they make arguments in favor of relativism.

To be sure, we must prove to the world that we are not narrow-minded, for narrow-mindedness is about attitude, not content. It is not narrow-minded to show someone that they are in error and that you hold the truth, but it is narrow-minded to become self-righteous about having the truth. It is narrow-minded to disrespect another person's humanity because you believe them to be in error. It is narrow-minded to question people's motives because they sincerely disagree with you.

Biblical Christians are not bigots merely because the claims of Christ are exclusive. For anyone to make such a claim is blatant bigotry. Christians are not imperialists just because they wish to engage in the marketplace of ideas. Why should anti-Christian voices be the only ones who are allowed to speak? Christians must stand up to every initiative to silence our voices in the public square or intimidate us from speaking the truth. On the contrary, we must be "ready always to give an answer to every man that asketh you a reason of the hope that is in you with meekness and fear" (1 Peter 3:15).

Divine Inclusion

Who are the beneficiaries of the saving work of Christ? The blessed ones are the babes (Matt. 11:25), people Jesus later calls those who "labour and are heavy laden" (11:28). It is the people who are humble enough to trust God who end up getting into the kingdom of God, not those who proudly reject any notion of the possibility of divine revelation. It is the weary, not the strong, who are included—the sinner, and not the self-righteous. Christianity is not designed for the benefit of high achievers but total failures.

Biblical Christianity thus has a glorious inclusiveness that no other religion shares. We have already established that in one sense it is very exclusive in its claims. But when coming to God through the Lord Jesus Christ, you are always welcomed, no matter who you are, where you have come from, how much you earn, what you look like, or whatever forms your identity. It is amazingly inclusive.

The inclusiveness of Christianity is so amazing that the world finds it hard to believe. Other religions only make room for high achievers, disciplined people, respectable people, and those who present themselves as being consistently pious and holy. In most religions, as well as in most of the secular world, egregious failure to meet their standards means that you are written off as a hopeless case. It is not so with Christ Jesus! The apostle Paul makes a long list of serious sins in 1 Corinthians 6:9–10: "Know ye not that the unrighteous shall not inherit the kingdom of God? Be not deceived: neither fornicators, nor idolaters, nor adulterers, nor effeminate, nor abusers of themselves with mankind, nor thieves, nor covetous, nor drunkards, nor revilers, nor extortioners, shall inherit the kingdom of God." Most of us are included somewhere in this list, either in thought, word, or deed. We are all outsiders to God's kingdom. But Paul is not done. In the very next verse, he says, "And such were some of you: but ye are washed, but ye are sanctified, but ye are justified in the name of the Lord Jesus, and by the Spirit of our God" (1 Cor. 6:11). That is how inclusive biblical Christianity is.

So many religions lack anything close to Christian compassion and forgiveness. They are rigid, cold, and condemning. If you are disciplined, if you are loving, if you are compassionate, if you are good, if you are moral, if you are decent, then perhaps you may be assured that you can please your god. If you are *not* all the above, however, you are out. There is justice without mercy. This is why so many false religions are immersed in hypocrisy—their devotees dare not admit that they are not perfect. They pretend to be shocked when people's flaws are exposed, and then they judge you.

With Christ, it is profoundly different. Authentic Christianity lets wicked people into God's kingdom, even at the last hour, like the penitent thief who hung on the cross next to Jesus (Luke 23:43). The world has no use for a religion that expunges the record of the vilest human beings who embrace Christ by faith, but that is the gospel. The world has no use for a religion that allows for the vicarious payment of an infinite debt by a substitute on behalf of a hopeless, worthless loser, but that is the message of the Bible. It is not the privileged, the wealthy, the connected, or the educated who are the focus of the gospel. This salvation is available to all who desperately need to be rescued from their sin and themselves. In the words of the apostle Paul,

> For ye see your calling, brethren, how that not many wise men after the flesh, not many mighty, not many noble, are called: but God hath chosen the foolish things of the world to confound the wise; and God hath chosen the weak things of the world to confound the things which are mighty; and base things of the world, and things which are despised, hath God chosen, yea, and things which are not, to bring to nought things that are: that no flesh should glory in his presence. But of him are ye in Christ Jesus, who of God is made unto us wisdom, and righteousness, and sanctification, and redemption: that, according as it is written, he that glorieth, let him glory in the Lord. (1 Corinthians 1:26–31)

In biblical Christianity, the welcome is for those who come with nothing, not those who have anything to boast about. We are not justified by our works here—we are in the kingdom solely because of the imputed righteousness of another.

What do we need to get into God's kingdom? Nothing! All we need is our need. If we are weary and burdened, we are welcomed in. The spiritual elite may not apply—not that they would want to—this is just for the babes. If we are prepared to put aside our spiritual credentials, then we will be welcomed in, just like all the other desperate sinners. Our salvation comes entirely from Christ. As the writer to the Hebrews says, "Wherefore he is able also to save them to the uttermost that come unto God by him, seeing he ever liveth to make intercession for them" (Heb. 7:25). Though our sins are as scarlet, they shall be white as snow; and though they are red like crimson, they shall be as wool (Isa. 1:18). On our worst days, we are never so despicable that we are beyond the reach of God's free grace. On our best days, we still need Christ's intercessory prayers on our behalf, and we will never outgrow our need of His grace.

God's Friends

How would you answer if someone asked you to give the purpose of religion? Is it about following a moral code and living the right way? Many think so. They are convinced that though all religions may have their own peculiarities and theological distinctives, ultimately, they all aim to keep us civil and respectful of each other. It is not just Christianity that talks about good behavior, morality, and ethics. Beautiful law codes in other religions encourage people to be civil and respectful of others, and even self-sacrificial in serving others. Some non-Christians may be more consistent with keeping certain of the Ten Commandments than professing Christians are. Indeed, many professing Christians regularly fall very short of what they profess to value. We should never boast about our morality and ethics as Christians. We are better advised to thank God for His restraining grace that keeps us from the most egregious activities into which we are regularly tempted to plunge.

If this is true, what makes biblical Christianity better than the alternatives? It is not merely that the moral teachings of Christ surpass the wisdom of every generation or that Christianity fosters joy and happiness in the hearts of believers. Nor is it simply that the Christian message provides comfort for those who are suffering and in need. All the above may be true, but they are not the essence of biblical Christianity. The essence of biblical Christianity is a deep intimacy with the Lord. Jesus Himself offers this invitation: "Take my yoke upon you, and learn of me; for I am meek and lowly in heart: and ye shall find rest unto your souls. For my yoke is easy, and my burden is light" (Matt. 11:29–30). Christianity is about knowing Jesus.

When our Lord called His disciples, He made the same point, saying, "Follow me" (Matt. 9:9). He never commanded them to follow this doctrine or that teaching. Rather, He said, "Follow me." He was calling them to know God intimately and personally. Knowing God is not the same as knowing about God. Knowing God means dealing with a person, not just an abstraction. You sense that God is opening your mind and pouring new truths in. You sense that God is speaking to your heart and that you are feeling His love pouring in. This is what our Lord Jesus prayed to the Father for on behalf of His people: "And this is life eternal, that they might know thee the only true God, and Jesus Christ, whom thou hast sent" (John 17:3). Knowing God through intimacy with Christ is what Christianity is all about.

Coming to know God changes your prayers—suddenly, prayer comes alive. In American football, when the situation becomes desperate and there seems no hope, the quarterback will throw a Hail Mary pass (a play apparently named after the Roman Catholic prayer). However, when you know God, prayers are never Hail Marys. When you come to know God, praying is not just praying to whatever gods there may be; it is not just throwing a petition out there into the void, hoping for the best. When you know God, you sense that when you pray, you are coming into the presence of your heavenly Father and that you know that He is yours and that you are His. You sense that He welcomes you. There is a sweet assurance and an intimacy that exists between you.

There is more. When you know God, you sense when He has come into your heart and is renovating you from the inside by His Spirit. Revolutionary things start happening in your inner being. You begin to understand things that you never understood before. You begin to see yourself becoming somebody you never thought you would ever become. A revolution has begun.

Let us return to Matthew 11:27: "And no man knoweth the Son, but the Father; neither knoweth any man the Father, save the Son, and he to whomsoever the Son will reveal him." This is a unique religious claim; no other religion offers anything quite like this. The Eastern faiths would never say that you can know God personally because, for them, God is an infinite force and not a person. The Muslims will admit to a personal God, but there is no intimacy with Allah. For them, God is too great and aloof to be anyone's friend. They would consider it the height of presumption to suggest that a man can know God intimately.

This explains the thick curtain that separated the holy of holies from the rest of the Jewish temple. Coming face-to-face with God meant certain death in the Old Testament. But something new has happened with the coming of Christ. Paul tells us, "For God, who commanded the light to shine out of darkness, hath shined in our hearts, to give the light of the knowledge of the glory of God in the face of Jesus Christ" (2 Cor. 4:6). Because of the work of Christ on behalf of elect sinners, we are no longer locked out of God's presence. On the contrary, "Having therefore, brethren, boldness to enter into the holiest by the blood of Jesus, by a new and living way, which he hath consecrated for us, through the veil, that is to say, his flesh; and having an high priest over the house of God; let us draw near with a true heart in full assurance of faith, having our hearts sprinkled from an evil conscience, and our bodies washed with pure water" (Heb. 10:19–22).

Because of Jesus alone, we are protected from the wrath of a holy God so that we who once were far off have now been brought near through the unmatched blood of the Lamb. Former enemies of God are now heirs of God and joint heirs with Christ, so that our status has changed. As the hymn writer put it,

> I once was an outcast stranger on earth,
> A sinner by choice, an alien by birth,
> But I've been adopted; my name's written down,
> An heir to a mansion, a robe, and a crown.[2]

If it is indeed true that the God of the Bible is the creator and sustainer of all things, and that the same God humbled Himself to become a part of His creation to redeem sinful man; if it is also true that He submitted to a painful and humiliating death for the benefit of elect sinners and He rose from the dead to authenticate His divinity and the efficacy of His blood; and if is also true that this resurrection confirms the future resurrection and eternal salvation of all recipients of His grace, then how can we withhold such truth from anyone on the planet? The challenge of the Christian missionary enterprise must be embraced, financed, promoted, and celebrated. We must shout this glorious gospel from the rooftops!

---

2. Hattie E. Buell, "A Child of the King," 1877.

Chapter 8

RADICAL MARRIAGE

Many in our generation, from within and without the church, both married and single, have thrown in the towel concerning marriage. Many who are married would be long gone from their marriage covenants if they did not have to deal with the guilt and shame of adversely affecting the children, disturbing the peace of their church, or upending their comfortable lifestyle. Many who are single have heard horror stories of marriage that have left them in a state of ambivalence—for the options of staying single, on the one hand, and marital stress on the other, do not seem attractive. Many in our generation are searching for someone to make sense of this institution called marriage, for it appears that we cannot live with it as individuals, and we cannot live without it as a society.

The Bible has a great deal to say about marriage. Genesis 2:18–25 is a famous passage that chronicles the first wedding on Earth and gives important insights into marriage's importance in the Holy Scriptures. The Bible begins in Genesis with the marriage of Adam and Eve, and it ends in the book of Revelation with a marriage between Christ, the Bridegroom, and His church, the bride. Marriage is an indispensable concept in redemptive history for understanding the work of Christ (see Eph. 5:22–33). This passage gives practical help to those who are looking for a godly spouse, as well as to those praying for healing or help with their marriage relationship. This passage also gives great hope to those who desire to establish a relationship with Christ, or who crave greater intimacy in their relationship with Christ, who is the Bridegroom of the church.

The Inevitable Struggle of Marriage

Many people have somehow acquired the notion that marriages are—or at least ought to be—conflict-free zones. For them, the presence of conflict is a sure sign that a marriage is sick. In reality, the opposite is often true—God has designed conflict in marriage. Genesis 2:18 says, "And the LORD God said, It is not good that the man should be alone; I will make him an help meet for him." The Hebrew word translated in this verse as *help* is regularly used in the Bible to refer to military reinforcements (see Deut. 33:29).[1] So, why is it being used here to describe a wife? The analogy is simple: in the context of a battle, when the enemy has the ascendancy, we are in a situation whose outcome depends on the timely arrival of such assistance. This characterization of the wife's contribution to her husband's life shows how highly valued she is—namely, the person most essential to his success in the journey through life.

She is more specifically described as a "help meet for him" (Gen. 2:18). She is not described as being *like* him but as *meet* for him, which means "corresponding to" or "suitable for." God designed husbands and wives to be both similar and different. Of course, the false narrative of our contemporary culture seeks to promote the similarities between the sexes at the expense of the differences. But what is clear from the biblical text is that what we have here is not a reference to an egalitarian relationship, or even a complementarian arrangement, but a benevolent patriarchy. The power dynamics do not have to be equal for a relationship to be satisfying. Both husband and wife are empowered in their unique ways, and the experience of most is that they will take turns possessing the ascendancy in any given situation. The important thing is not that they maintain equal power at all times—or any particular time—but that both parties are allowed to thrive and grow, enjoying the acceptance of love, even in the context of the struggle.

In other words, what is happening in marriage is the reality of two sinners willingly consenting to be joined together for life, to love

---

1. Dan B. Allender and Tremper Longman III, *Intimate Allies* (Wheaton, Ill.: Tyndale House Publishers, 1995), 148.

and serve each other according to their God-given natures and roles, and to patiently endure the radical differences in each other's idiosyncrasies, tastes, opinions, dreams, experiences, and backgrounds. This is not a formula for perpetual tranquility; this is a struggle. But it is a struggle that is welcomed and embraced. Those committed to Christ ultimately agree that they would rather struggle together to forge an authentic intimacy than take the easy and unsatisfying path of shallow and transient relationships.

One of the problems of marriage in our culture is consumerism. There is something fundamentally wrong when we start talking about our relationships as if we were acquiring goods and services in the marketplace. The culture considers marriage as a product that must gratify our immediate feelings. We have described the struggle of marriage as a good thing, but most of us do not want a product that pushes back. The complexity of marriage is a turnoff for many people who have embraced the delusion that true love is—or at least ought to be—conflict free. As soon as they discover that they are dealing with another sinner like them, they are ready to run away. Discipled by the Burger King motto, their slogan is, "I want to have it my way." The only problem with this kind of thinking is that it is far from reality. None of us gets to have it our way in any real relationship. The struggle is the divinely prescribed context for nurturing intimacy with our spouses as well as with our God. The confrontations are the exercise program that strengthen our relational and spiritual muscles.

One of the fallacious assumptions that is common in our generation is the idea that there is someone out there who is the right person for us, and all we have to do is look around and wait until we find them. To the contrary, Stanley Hauerwas has argued that, in fact, we are always destined to marry the wrong person.[2] After all, we never really know the people we marry when we marry them; we just think we do. What is more, even if we are pretty sure we have married the right person, people change. Marriage itself has such an effect on us

---

2. Stanley Hauerwas, "Sex and Politics: Bertrand Russell and 'Human Sexuality,'" *Christian Century* XCV, no. 14 (April 19, 1978): 417–22.

that we are not the same people after entering it. As a result, all those who are searching for a conflict-free marriage are deluded. Butting heads is inevitable in marriage, and if we persist long enough, we will see that this is actually the refiner's fire intended to remove the dross from our lives and make us pure gold (see Mal. 3:2–4).

The struggle is both inevitable and sanctifying, as it exposes our sins and calls us to pursue real change. The problem is that many people do not persevere long enough to benefit from the struggle. We have allowed ourselves to become too swallowed up in romantic naivety. Instead, we need to allow the Word of God to call us back to reality and encourage us to embrace the struggle.

Idolatrous Self-Righteousness in Marriage

Genesis 2 gives us an inspired description of the first wedding. In our Western culture, the father brings the bride down the aisle and gives her to the groom. In this case, the father of the bride is none other than the Lord God Almighty. The Almighty brought Eve, the first bride, and gave her to her groom, Adam. When Adam saw Eve, he exploded into poetry. I read somewhere that, "Some people are artists, but others, themselves, are art." Eve was a magnificent work of art—the first piece of art in the history of the world.

When a man sees a woman and bursts into poetry, he is profoundly smitten. When Adam said, "This is now bone of my bones, and flesh of my flesh" (Gen. 2:23), the thrust of his statement was, "At last! This is what I have been looking for; this completes me!" Adam had named all the animals and not found a suitable companion (v. 20). Now, however, he was testifying that just seeing this beautiful woman had given him insights into his own nature and being. Eve was more than just human being number two; like a lock in the presence of a key, she made sense of his existence, defined his purpose as a man, and presented hope for personal fulfillment. This illustrates the absurdity and perversion of homosexuality, which can be summarized simply as *mission impossible*. It is utter foolishness to celebrate the so-called civil rights of a key, then embrace another key as if it were a lock.

The perversion of homosexuality is illogical and unproductive, as well as spiritually disastrous. But we are perhaps in greater danger of falling for a different perversion: the idolatrous exaltation of a person of the opposite sex, whether they are a prospective spouse or even a spouse. Like Adam, we can start to elevate a person to the point that our relationship moves from romance to worship and forget that we already have a God who is our creator and sustainer, a God who has holy jealousy. Sometimes we might be sitting on the precipice of eternal perdition, not because we have a terrible marriage, but because we have a good one. If we adore any man or woman more than we adore our God, or if our focus on any man or woman eclipses our view of and our obligations to our maker, we will eventually destroy both our relationship with God and our relationship with this person who has become an idol (see Matt. 10:37). Every marriage needs the sobriety of regularly reaffirming that no man or woman must ever take the holy place of God. Adam's legitimate romance with Eve eventually became perverted and turned into a wicked idolatry that led him to obey his wife's word instead of the word of God (Gen. 3:6).

Some of us may be tempted to think that such idolatrous obsession with our spouse or prospective spouse is impossible for us because the relationship is already flawed or even miserable. We think, "I do not believe I am about to idolize that fool any time soon." But this thinking is erroneous. True, one may not have a great marriage right now, and one may not be currently idolizing and worshiping their spouse. But the reason for what appear to be irreconcilable marital difficulties may be that the relationship began and has continued with idolatrous expectations which have upended whatever intimacy existed between a couple. Repentance may be in order. We must be deliberate in rejecting the worldly paradigm of looking to our spouse to give us the things only God can provide.

All married sinners must admit that they have contributed to the problems in their marriages by having idolatrous expectations. We have been utterly unreasonable in our expectation that our spouse's love, respect, affirmation, sexuality, and so forth should give meaning to our lives and bring us continual joy and satisfaction. Only God can do that. But the result of this idolatry is that we are often ready to trade in our spouses for a newer model if they fall short of giving us what only God can. How unreasonable!

Our quest for meaning in life and even a sense of personal value are things that we can only get from God. There is only one Savior, and His name is not darling, sweetheart, or honey. The Lord God alone can save us, for He is the only potentate, King of Kings and Lord of Lords. We need to give our spouses a break and instead look to the true and living God for salvation and meaning in our lives. No human relationship can bear the weight of those kinds of expectations.

None of us is perfect. Yet very often when it comes to our spouses, we completely forget this. So, we demand perfection—we forget that they are sinners like us and demand that they consistently behave like God, which is the definition of idolatry. We have a deluded picture in our minds of absolute blissful love in marriage, and we decide that we cannot settle for anything less than this fantasy. We regularly tolerate mediocrity and imperfection in almost every other area of life while we strive for improvement, but not with our marriages. If it is not immediately perfect, blissful, and perpetually romantic, we stand ready to abandon the covenant we made before God.

This idolatry is not simply manifested among the married; it is found even among single people. Unmarried people make an idol out of marriage by becoming overly discriminating in their evaluations of spousal prospects. No one seems good enough for them. Even though they know that they are not perfect, they often demand that potential spouses must be perfect—they must be like God. Such thinking is from la-la land; it is idolatry. We are never to have low standards, but neither are we to entertain unrealistic and self-righteous expectations. While we encourage growth and maturity in our spouses, let us never throw our spouses under the bus simply because they have not arrived at our demanded level of moral, emotional, and spiritual perfection. None of us will ever find a perfect spouse, and neither will anyone who finds us. God alone is the one we must look to for perfection, salvation, and ultimate fulfillment. Jesus Christ is the only lover who will never let us down.

Marriage as a Picture of Salvation

Genesis 2:24–25 outlines the fundamentals of what God expects from a marital union. There are at least four expectations here. We are (1) to leave our parents and create a new family unit, (2) to cleave to our spouse and create a new exclusive intimacy, (3) to become one flesh with our spouse and merge our lives into a single identity, and (4) to be naked with our spouse, working for total openness in covenant security. But it is much more than all of the above. When the apostle Paul explains this text in the New Testament, it becomes abundantly clear that human marriage is pedagogical—it teaches and illustrates the ultimate marriage, the saving work of Christ, the ultimate Bridegroom, in coming to the rescue of His beloved bride, the church (Eph. 5:22–33).

Christ is the prototype of a husband's matrimonial initiative. Every husband should leave his father and mother because Christ left the Father in the covenant of redemption to rescue the remnant according to grace. Every husband should cleave to his wife because Christ established an everlasting bond and a mystical union with His chosen bride, the elect of every nation, promising never to leave or forsake them. Every husband should think of himself as one flesh with his bride because Christ has caused His bride, the church, to become heirs of God and joint heirs with Him, even as His bride is united to Him. Every husband should be willing to become emotionally naked with his bride because of Christ's self-giving: "Who, being in the form of God, thought it not robbery to be equal with God: but made himself of no reputation, and took upon him the form of a servant, and was made in the likeness of men: and being found in fashion as a man, he humbled himself, and became obedient unto death, even the death of the cross" (Phil. 2:6–8).

We need to have God in our lives, not merely as the object of our faith or the ruler of our lives; we need Him as our spouse. Because of the *imago Dei*, we have something in common with our God. While His image in us has been defaced by sin, it has not been erased. We are mirrors that reflect His glory in every environment of our lives. But while we identify with Him in the sense that we mirror His glory as His image bearers, we are not like Him at all in another sense, for He is infinitely holy. Like Moses, we sing, "Who is like unto thee, O LORD, among the gods? who is like thee, glorious in holiness, fearful in praises, doing wonders?" (Ex. 15:11).

It is with this God that true believers have entered a marriage covenant. As different as this divine Bridegroom, our Lord Jesus, is from His frail and tainted bride, the church, nonetheless, "Christ also loved the church, and gave himself for it; that he might sanctify and cleanse it with the washing of water by the word, that he might present it to himself a glorious church, not having spot, or wrinkle, or any such thing; but that it should be holy and without blemish" (Eph. 5:25–27).

We will never become the righteous people we are supposed to be unless the Lord God comes into our lives as a spouse, not just as a kind of abstract principle of love, or as somebody we obey from a distance. The Lord God has to be in our lives as our lover, which means that He has to be in our lives intimately. There has to be interaction through prayer, through listening to His Word, and through passionate worship. He has to be in our life through the ordinary means of grace. We will never become the people that we ought to be unless that is the case. Our God is the ultimate spousal relationship that we need, the one that will inform and transform our earthly marriage.

What are the implications of such intimacy? We cannot claim to have entered into a covenant with the true and living God and then turn around and live for our career, our money, our social calendar, our political connections, or anything else. That would be spiritual adultery. This happens when we give our hearts' deepest passions and love to someone or something besides God. Our God has a sense of betrayal and grief far more significant than we would feel if our human spouse were unfaithful to us. This is because He is perfect in everything, even His grief. Because of our sin, we are all the ultimate spouses from hell, cheaters of the worst kind, yet our God is the ultimate faithful Bridegroom, making His bride beautiful in spite of herself.

Jesus Christ came into this world in order to win back His wayward bride, to woo her into returning home. But we did not just spurn and reject Him; we nailed Him to the cross. As Jesus anticipated the cross in the garden of Gethsemane, He knew what agony and alienation it would take for Him to stay and love us to the end. Yet He stayed the course. Here is the ultimate spousal love. Christ is the spouse with no illusions—He never expects us to be perfect in this world. Jesus loves His bride, not because we are lovely or lovable, nor because we are going to give Him so much affirmation. He loves us just because He loves us—in order to make us loveable through His perfect life and atoning death in our place! This is true love of the highest kind. As Charles Wesley put it,

> Love divine, all loves excelling,
> Joy of heav'n, to earth come down,
> Fix in us Thy humble dwelling;
> All Thy faithful mercies crown.
> Jesus, Thou art all compassion;
> Pure, unbounded love Thou art;
> Visit us with Thy salvation;
> Enter ev'ry trembling heart.[3]

The Bible begins with a wedding. This wedding's original purpose was to fill the world with true worshipers of God, but it failed to accomplish that goal because the husband in that marriage was unwilling to step in and help his wife when she needed him to lead. He, instead, followed her to their ruin (see Gen. 3:1–6). At the end of time, however, there will be another wedding. This is the marriage supper of the Lamb, and its purpose is also to fill the world with true worshipers of God—the true Israel of God, the elect of every nation—and it will succeed where the first marriage failed. This second marriage will succeed because the second husband is the author of perfection and is the very incarnation of God, and as such, He can never fail! The second Adam, the faithful Adam, Jesus Christ our Lord, will never let down His bride. He has not; He does not; and He will not. As Lowell Mason wrote,

> O Royal Bride give heed,
> And to my words attend;

---

3. Charles Wesley, "Love Divine, All Loves Excelling," 1747.

For Christ the King forsake the world
And ev'ry former friend.

Thy beauty and thy grace
Shall then delight the King;
He only is the rightful Lord,
To Him thy worship bring.

To thee, since thou art His,
Great honor shall be shown;
The rich shall bring their gifts to thee
Thy glory they shall own.

Enthroned in royal state,
All glorious thou shalt dwell,
With garments fair, in-wrought with gold,
The Church He loveth well.[4]

True believers in Christ should wholeheartedly agree that "marriage is not so much finding the right person as it is being the right person."[5] Take the godly advice of 1 Corinthians 13:4–7 and let us be the right person: "Charity suffereth long, and is kind; charity envieth not; charity vaunteth not itself, is not puffed up, doth not behave itself unseemly, seeketh not her own, is not easily provoked, thinketh no evil; rejoiceth not in iniquity, but rejoiceth in the truth; beareth all things, believeth all things, hopeth all things, endureth all things."

---

4. Lowell Mason, "The Church, the Bride of Christ," 1912.
5. Charles W. Shedd, *Letters to Karen* (Nashville, Tenn.: Abingdon Press, 1965), 13.

Chapter 9

RADICAL LABOR

Do you look forward to going to work every day? Is your work a reluctant duty, or is it a welcome responsibility? We often demonstrate the true nature of our hearts in our reason for working and our manner of working. This can tell us whether we have a healthy or pathological relationship with God. Our work can be a blessing, but it can also become an albatross around our necks. It can be marked with productivity and faithful stewardship on the one hand or a painful, cursed daily experience on the other.

One of the great surprises for many people is discovering that God always intended for us to work. The eternal state of the new heavens and the new earth will not be a place of idleness and zero productivity. From the garden of Eden to the eternal state in glory, God has always had work for us to do. Work is not the product of sin. But sin has corrupted work. Genesis 2 gives us the biblical perspective on work, the labor of our hands. As a result, studying this foundational passage is essential to grasping and embracing a genuinely biblical work ethic.

The Standing of Work
Genesis 2:7–8 not only tells us that God created man from the dust of the ground but also that God sent him into the world to work that ground from which he came. God dignified the status of work by setting the example—He planted a garden, then He placed the man in it to work it and take care of it (2:15). Our ideas about work today have been influenced, to a large extent, by ancient Greco-Roman

attitudes. In the Greco-Roman world, manual labor was considered demeaning. The Greeks believed that the material world was essentially evil and that the spiritual world was good. So, in this paradigm, noble work was any kind of work that did not involve the use of your hands and thus kept you away from matter. As a result, work such as philosophy or poetry was considered ennobling, while any kind of physical work was considered demeaning and even dehumanizing.

This Greco-Roman perspective, practically ubiquitous today in the Western world, is seriously challenged by this passage at the beginning of the book of Genesis. Here we have the God of glory with His hands in the dirt. God is revealed to be a manual laborer, planting a garden with His hands in the dust. Moreover, when we get to the New Testament, we see God not just simply coming into contact with the physical world but actually becoming physical in the person of our Lord Jesus Christ when He became incarnate, actually receiving a body. Then, we see God the Father raising Jesus from the dead, resurrecting the body. In Romans 8:11, we are told that God will eventually redeem even the bodies of true disciples of Christ, not just our souls.

This is a remarkable statement of the dignity of all work, whether it is blue collar or white collar. All work brings order out of chaos in some way or other and in that way mimics the Creator. God was the first to bring order out of chaos. The creation narrative explains that the Spirit of God moved across the face of the waters (Gen. 1:2). Everything was without form and void, literally chaos, until God spoke, and everything changed (1:3). Then God proceeded to put people in the garden of Eden with a mandate to continue the work of bringing order out of chaos. They were to take the natural raw material, the soil, and the various plants and to cultivate them into something beautiful and valuable (2:15). God dignified work in all its forms, even manual labor. Work was not invented because of sin; rather, work was corrupted and complicated by sin (3:17–19). We were always meant to work, not merely to laze around.

Ordinary physical and material life is good in itself. This physical world is not just a temporary means to a spiritual end. It has intrinsic value. Our salvation does not require the jettisoning of the material; it embraces the physical. The God of the Bible took a body, permitted it to be killed as a sacrifice, resurrected it, and promised to redeem the bodies of His people. Scripture teaches us that there is going to be a new heaven and a new earth (Rev. 21:1). We will all be great gardeners in the paradise of our God, for in God's economy, there are no second-class jobs. The physical, the material, is celebrated and given high standing by the God of glory, the Ancient of Days, who created it in the first place.

This esteem for work in God's economy suggests that we need a paradigm shift in our culture's perspective on work. How we do our work matters, for, "Every man's work shall be made manifest: for the day shall declare it, because it shall be revealed by fire; and the fire shall try every man's work of what sort it is" (1 Cor. 3:13). It matters that we do honest work: "Let him that stole steal no more: but rather let him labour, working with his hands the thing which is good, that he may have to give to him that needeth" (Eph. 4:28). Our time management matters to God: "See then that ye walk circumspectly, not as fools, but as wise, redeeming the time, because the days are evil (Eph. 5:15–16). It matters that we earn our own way in this world and are not dependent on others: "For even when we were with you, this we commanded you, that if any would not work, neither should he eat" (2 Thess. 3:10). Our work ethic impacts our Christian testimony: "But if any provide not for his own, and specially for those of his own house, he hath denied the faith, and is worse than an infidel" (1 Tim. 5:8).

The Stewardship of Work

In Genesis 2:15, we are told something about the nature of work. It is clear from the passage that gardening is the paradigm for defining and evaluating work. We must not forget that the first man, Adam, represented the whole human race. Therefore, anything God asked him to do speaks to and clarifies the responsibilities of the entire human race. Thus, gardening serves as a model and template for all forms of work. Gardeners change the environment radically. The purpose is never destruction but rather a sustainable development that respects the environment and improves the lives of everyone. The gardener may cut down some trees and pull up plants that are in the wrong place and replace them with others that are more suited to that spot. The goal is to produce a beautiful and harmonious place of rest.

When we go to work, we similarly aim to rearrange the raw material of a particular domain to draw out its potential for human flourishing. We are fools if we end up destroying the environment, or if we allow it to develop without order and any benefit to anyone. Conservation and development must be held in a delicate balance. Our challenge is to be respectfully creative with our environment. Thus, we will clear the ground so that the sun can come in and allow us to produce the food that will nourish our bodies and the flowers that encourage our souls.

All work is like that. For example, a musician takes the twelve notes on the keyboard as their raw material and creates with them something that will enrich us all. Music is taking the raw material of sound, which is part of our physical world, and reshaping it so that when we hear it, it brings meaning and beauty to our lives. The musician's garden is the field of sound. In this sense, we are all gardeners, no matter what field we are in. We are all gardeners in God's field, whether preaching, teaching, selling, building, managing, serving, accounting, assessing, planning, nurturing, cleaning, entertaining, or defending. Our stewardship of the resources matters to God. We are given the mandate by God to tame the natural world, including all the raw materials, in a responsible way that will enhance and enrich the lives of everyone in a sustainable manner (Gen. 1:28). God created all these domains, and He puts us in them so that we may creatively and graciously rearrange them for human flourishing.

The God of the Bible has a powerful work ethic. In eternity, He was God all by Himself in His triune glory as Father, Son, and Holy Spirit. He had infinite resources and potential, including love, personality, community, and glory. God did not hoard His unlimited resources to Himself. Rather, He decided to rescue His elect, leveraging His resources to create space for a whole universe of beings to share the riches that He had from all eternity, even though it would cost Him dearly.

In like manner, when each of us sees a need in our society that has not been filled, God is calling and challenging us to find the talent and ability somewhere around us that could fill it. We are challenged to leverage our resources to produce a product that keeps on giving value to the lives of everyone. This is not only godly but also godlike, mimicking the maker. We fulfill our call to be image bearers of our God when we are at work, rearranging a particular domain to bring blessing to those around us.

Of course, this is not the general view of our generation. Many continue to view work as a means of achieving a particular socioeconomic standing. They are only interested in how their work may aid upward mobility. In no way are they thinking about the dignity of all work, nor do they think about work in terms of impact and service to others. If we become doctors, it should be because of a deep interest in relieving suffering. If we become lawyers, it should be because of a deep passion for justice. If we become pastors, it should be because of a deep sense of calling to advance the gospel of Christ to the saving of souls. If we become farmers, it should be because of a deep sense of responsibility to feed the hungry. Whatever we become should never be driven simply by dreams of money or prestige. This will only lead to overwork, boredom, emptiness, and even indifference. This inevitably hurts both productivity and purpose.

Joy and happiness in our work does not result from work done merely for the remuneration package or the retirement benefits. There is no satisfaction in work that is done merely for social standing or upward mobility. Our work will be pleasing when it is done for the good of all—work that is truly a gracious expression of creative energy in the service of others. In the same way, we are set up for failure, disappointment, and futility if we are looking to our work to give us our identity, our sense of significance, or our security. In that case, our work has become an idol. Let the work be about the work, creatively meeting needs for the good of all in a sustainable manner. Instead of idolizing our work, we need to recognize that we are stewards of the gifts and talents God has given us. As 1 Corinthians 4:2 reminds us, "Moreover it is required in stewards, that a man be found faithful." Let us rise to the challenge of faithful stewardship to the glory of our God—a stewardship that causes others to see our good work and glorify our Father which is in heaven, a stewardship that causes those who come behind us to find us faithful, and a stewardship of which we have no need to be ashamed on the day of the Lord.

The Staining of Work

There is an explicit prohibition in Genesis 2:17 about eating from a particular tree, which came with a warning about immediate, drastic, and cosmic consequences: "For in the day that thou eatest thereof thou shalt surely die." Of course, the narrative of the next chapter, Genesis 3, tells us of the advent of sin and the fall of humanity. It is evident from the narrative that our first parents did not instantly perish with their transgression. But it soon becomes clear as we go through the Scriptures that death is more than merely physical. Death is the incremental and inevitable deterioration of everything around us and in us. We are all falling apart and so is everything in this world associated with us. It does not matter how hard we work, exercise, or participate in cosmetic or surgical adjustments. We are all dying.

This death is much more than physical; it is at work socially, culturally, vocationally, and spiritually. Everything is falling apart. Death descended upon us when we lost our covenant relationship with God, and it is gradually eating everything up—including our work. That is why, even though work continues, it is now impeded by thorns, drought, floods, pests, fatigue, stress, and fruitlessness. While the doctrine of creation rebukes a cynical attitude about the dignity of our work, the doctrine of the fall kills all romantic notions concerning our work. The former reminds us that all kinds of work matter and should be respected. The latter reminds us that our work now involves drudgery that we must all undergo in order to meet our responsibilities and pay our bills.

The frustration of work takes a variety of different forms. When we are young, we have a lot of stamina and idealism—we think we are going to change the world through our labors. But while we are young, we often lack the wisdom to know how to address profound problems. By the time we eventually learn such wisdom, we are exhausted and old, unable to accomplish the task we now know how to do. In the same way, putting a team together, building a brand, developing a concept, and implementing a vision or plan takes time. But it does not take much time at all for someone in the project to rebel and sabotage the whole thing. Construction takes hard work in order to achieve a goal that is a sustainable blessing to all, but demolition is often indifferent to concerns about purpose, respect, and dignity. If the Lord is not involved in our work, it is an exercise in futility—busyness without any serious business. As the psalmist reminds us, "Except the LORD build the house, they labour in vain that build it: except the LORD keep the city, the watchman waketh but in vain" (Ps. 127:1).

Despite sin's assault on work—staining it and corrupting its purpose—our God still calls us to vocational integrity. While we mourn the frustrations caused by sin, we can still celebrate the usefulness of work for our sanctification. With this hope, we may join the hymnwriter in this celebration of work:

> Work, for the night is coming,
> Work through the sunny noon;
> Fill brightest hours with labor,
> Rest comes sure and soon.
> Give every flying minute,
> Something to keep in store;
> Work, for the night is coming,
> When man works no more.[1]

The Saving of Work

In Antigua and Barbuda, where I live, the Labor Code spells out a mandatory minimum of twelve days per annum of vacation for workers. Employers may choose to give additional vacation days

---

1. Annie L. Coghill, "Work for the Night is Coming," 1854.

or weeks according to the years of service for their employees. Of course, this is all subject to the nature of the work done by a given organization, whether the enterprise is for-profit or non-profit. Yet one way or another, employees in Antigua and Barbuda have to work for their rest. This system makes us earn our vacation.

The Word of God has it the other way around. Our God offers us deep rest as a free gift, which enables us to do our work correctly. The first two chapters of Genesis describe the various days of creation. Six of these days are described as having evening and morning. There is, however, a striking difference between these six days and the seventh day. On the seventh day, it says that God rested and there is no mention of evening and morning (Gen. 2:1–3). The absence of evening and morning for the seventh day suggests that this day has never ended. Indeed, Hebrews 4:9–10 declares, "There remaineth therefore a rest to the people of God. For he that is entered into his rest, he also hath ceased from his own works, as God did from his." This resting of the people of God from their work obviously does not mean that we are not to have jobs. Rather, it frees us from finding our identity and meaning in life through our work.

We have all watched or participated in the rat race of the workplace. We see people jockeying for position, hoping to open the door of success and get that break that will separate them from everyone else. Employees and bosses run around, working their fingers to the bone. They may tell themselves that they are burning the candle on both ends for the sake of their wives and families, for the children they scarcely ever see. They insist that church attendance must wait, for their work requires their undivided attention and priority. Yet, in reality, they are trying to prove themselves through their work.

Because of what we lost through the sin of our first parents in the garden of Eden, many of us have bowed to the idol of work and are looking to our careers—and not to our God—to give us our identity, our sense of significance, and our sense of security. Before the fall, our first parents stood before the face of God and knew Him. We stood there too, for we were in them as our covenant heads. Through this intimacy with God, man found his identity, significance, and security because he was created as an image bearer of God. He knew who he was. He knew that he had value and security in God. It was clear to him why he went to work, which had nothing to do with earning his identity, significance, and security. Now, because of our sin, we have lost all that. We are seeking to find it elsewhere—for many of us, through our work. Yet, in reality, we find nothing but frustration and emptiness there. It is not the actual labor of our work that wears us out, resulting in burnout and breakdowns. It is the hard work of expecting to receive from our work what only God can give us: our true identity and the source of our significance and security.

The author of Hebrews calls us to rest from our work. He invites us to experience a deep sense that our God loves us and that our life counts. Only then will we be able to move out into the workplace and seek to serve others, for our work will no longer be about our insecurities and anxieties; it will be about the gracious expression of the gifts God has given us in the service of others in a sustainable way.

How do we get that rest of which the writer to the Hebrews speaks? The key is in Genesis 2:3, where God pronounced the end of His work of creation by announcing the Sabbath of rest: "And God blessed the seventh day, and sanctified it: because that in it he had rested from all his work which God created and made." The work was finished. In like manner, at the end of the work of redemption, our Lord Jesus Christ declared His work complete just before He died, "After this, Jesus knowing that all things were now accomplished, that the scripture might be fulfilled, saith, I thirst. Now there was set a vessel full of vinegar: and they filled a spunge with vinegar, and put it upon hyssop, and put it to his mouth. When Jesus therefore had received the vinegar, he said, It is finished: and he bowed his head, and gave up the ghost" (John 19:28–30). Jesus's work of redemption was designed to end our work of futility. Because of His work—when He lived the life for us that we should have lived, and died the death for us that we should have died—because of all that He did to guarantee for us a right relationship with God, we can now experience that deep rest for our souls that He promised. We can now work for the glory of God and the good of others. Our work will no longer be idolatry, the hopeless expectation that our labor will give us what only God can provide.

This rest is also a rest of hope. In this life, we have many unfulfilled goals and dreams. We are constantly sighing with regret for lost years and missed opportunities. We reluctantly settle for less, accepting the cold, brutal reality of a world of disappointment. But because of this promised rest in Christ, we have hope. All the beautiful things that are in our hearts right now, the things that are obviously from God, the things that we desire to accomplish that will glorify Him and bless the church—all these things will be achieved in God's perfect environment, the paradise to come. On that day, we will get the deep rest of hope and peace and at the same time be able to do our work to the honor and glory of our God.

According to the humorist Evan Esar, there is only one thing worse than living without working, and that is to work without living. Living without working leaves you with a sense of personal uselessness, while working without living leaves you with a sense of lost opportunity, vanity, and futility. The Christian work ethic brings us into balance. The high standing of work is affirmed by divine example in planting a garden; the stewardship of work is pursued with the desire to meet needs of others creatively for the good of all; the staining of work warns us against the danger of idolatry. The saving of work is secured as it is put in the context of the glorious work of Christ, which guarantees that our labors are not in vain (1 Cor. 15:58).

With this gospel, we can join Fanny Crosby who wrote,

> To the work! to the work! we are servants of God,
> Let us follow the path that our Master has trod;
> With the might of His power our strength to renew,
> Let us do by His grace what He calls us to do.
>
> Toiling on, toiling on, toiling on, toiling on;
> Let us hope, and trust, let us watch, and pray,
> And labor till the Master comes.[2]

---

2. Fanny Crosby, "To the Work!", 1869.

Chapter 10

RADICAL PERSPECTIVE

In Psalm 27, David brings up some rather negative themes. Such negativity is not widely fashionable in our day. Many people would suggest that it is more helpful to think about positive ideas and developments. Yet David testifies here that facing up to the negative realities of life did not lead him to despair. Instead, he was able to testify to the contrary, "I had fainted, unless I had believed to see the goodness of the LORD in the land of the living" (Ps. 27:13). How was David able to face up squarely to the negativity of life in a fallen world and still end up with doxology?

This psalm addresses our tendency to be consumed with fear, worry, and anxiety. We have biblical guidance here about how to deal with this problem, while maintaining a refreshing realism. David invokes a variety of contexts that have the potential to produce great anxiety in his life, but he responds to each one with an unshakable faith in the God of his fathers. For example, he says, "When my father and my mother forsake me, then the LORD will take me up" (v. 10). There is no indication, however, that David's parents had actually forsaken him. Likewise, David envisaged an entire army being encamped against him (v. 6), even before that possibility became a present reality. He was visualizing the worst things that could happen to him in order to establish a strategy of dealing with his fears and anxieties in a manner that would stand up to anything.

David did not accept the popular notion that we should always think positively and never spend time imagining the worst. His strategy—inspired by the Holy Spirit—was to take on the threats to our peace head-on. The God of the Bible desires that we address our anger, anxiety, and fear, in all their forms, by applying an unswerving faith in God even before those scenarios are played out in our experience. The God of the Bible wants us to anticipate and harness the negative events in our lives for the glory of God and our good.

Many in our generation, especially in Western nations, are obsessed with emotional threats and demand that the world give them "safe spaces" in order to guard their fragile psychological makeup against being "triggered." The problems of the psalmist, David, were far more serious than many of our modern concerns. Brutal enemies were plotting to assassinate him and take over his kingdom. Yet he faced up to these difficulties with great confidence in the Lord.

David's approach can be summed up in three verbs in verse 4: to *dwell*, to *behold*, and to *inquire*. This verse says, "One thing have I desired of the LORD, that will I seek after; that I may dwell in the house of the LORD all the days of my life, to behold the beauty of the LORD, and to enquire in his temple." The same strategy will enable us to face the anxieties and stresses in our own lives. We must not seek to run away from reality; rather, we must face our challenges within the context of God's promises of grace and redemption.

To Be in His Presence

The psalmist is abundantly clear that his primary request of the Lord is to *dwell* in the Lord's house (vv. 4–6). David was not thinking about a physical location when he said that. He could not dwell in the house of the Lord in a literal sense, for living in the temple was restricted to the Levites. Indeed, the holy of holies was out of bounds for everyone except the high priest, and even he could only enter once per year (Heb. 9:7). David was thus not asking to make the temple his physical residence. Rather, what he was asking for was to experience the uninterrupted presence of God. This was his sole ambition—to see God's very face and be always in His presence.

That may sound strange to us at first. Is it not true that God is present everywhere? The explanation lies in the difference between acquaintance and intimacy—that is, in the difference between cursory knowledge and intimate knowledge. The face is, after all, the relational gateway into the heart. It is generally not easy to nurture long-distance relationships, even with today's social media. In the days before social media, it was much harder. I tried it while at university in Oklahoma in the early 1980s, but I almost lost the young lady in Antigua and Barbuda who eventually became my wife because we could not afford the overseas telephone calls.

Above all, we long to see a person's face. When we meet somebody, we should not look at their feet or their shoulders. We should look into their face if we want to have an authentic personal transaction. It is with the face that we see and hear each other. In Psalm 19:1, we are told that the heavens declare the glory of God. That is, they give us accurate information and revelation about God. But looking up at the stars does not give us a personal and intimate experience of God. Nature cannot do that. We have to come before God face-to-face. David's desire was not to know God from a distance, or in a general way; he wanted to see the face of God so that his interactions with God could be personal and intimate.

David's desire to dwell in God's house and gaze on God's beauty in Psalm 27:4 was the source of his confident peace in verse 3: "My heart shall not fear." He was teaching us that our fears are directly proportional to the vulnerability of the things that are our greatest joys. If our greatest joy is God, then we will live without fear. If our primary desire is to be with God, then we are safe. David is not suggesting that he would be physically safer inside the tabernacle—the people pursuing him with swords would not have been deterred by him running inside a building. Rather, his security was wrapped up in whatever he desired the most. We are only safe when it is God that we want the most—not even the blessings of God, but God Himself.

Anxiety comes into our hearts whenever we foolishly elevate finite things to the status of the infinite in our devotion and attention. These finite things are not necessarily bad in themselves; on the contrary, they are often good things like family, career, romance, sex, entertainment, and property. The problem comes when these good things become the one thing we think that we must have to be happy. So we adore them and believe we cannot receive life joyfully unless we have them. Our idolatry occurs when we take these good things and pervert them by worshiping them. We turn them into inordinate desires, which in turn creates the anxiety that paralyzes us. Anxiety is often the result of the implosion or impending collapse of a false god. When the *one thing* that we have to have is threatened and seems about to be lost, the result is fear and anxiety.

In reality, everything in this life except God and His will is subject to the vicissitudes of time and therefore vulnerable. Nothing, however, can take God away from us; He is never vulnerable. All other things—people, achievements, aspirations, and experiences—can be taken away from us, but when our hearts are set on God and God alone, we become invincible and fearless. As a result, our anxiety is actually beneficial to us, for if we follow our worries to their source, we can often identify what is enslaving us and what we have made into our idol. Our idol is the passionate dream of our hearts and the thing that occupies most of our time. It is our constant longing at the midnight hour, the primary focus of our spending, the principal lusting of our hearts, and the main topic of our conversations. When that one thing collapses or is threatened, we start to become fearful and afraid.

Gazing on the Lord

The central phrase in verses 7–10 of Psalm 27 is, "Thy face, LORD, will I seek," which is found in verse 8. These words describe what the verb *behold* in verse 4 is all about. Having established what he desired from the Lord, David went after it with all his faculties; he involved himself with intensive meditation. So too, when we are in the presence of God, our immediate duty is to gaze on His beauty, to behold His radiance.

What does it mean to behold God's beauty? This is what the Christian church has called communion with God. It is the difference between knowing about God and knowing God. It is the difference between *knowing* that God is holy and loving, on the one hand, and personally *experiencing* God's holiness and love, on the other. The church father Augustine divided meditation into three aspects: retaining, contemplating, and delighting in the Lord. This is how we behold His beauty.

First, we must retain the truth of God—that is, we must learn it, hold on to it, and master it. We must diligently seek out and gather the truth about God from the Scriptures. This is foundational, but it is not enough. Our gaze has just begun. We must then contemplate—that is, we study that truth about God for applications to our lives. We ask how these truths impact our relationship with God and our fellow men and women. We must let the truth inform our thinking, affections, and actions, changing us from the inside out. Even then, we are not finished with gazing upon God.

We cannot be emotionally unaffected when we genuinely retain and contemplate God's revelation of Himself. We cannot remain indifferent and apathetic if we genuinely discern who God is. The revelation of God's truth, the portrait of His majesty in the unveiling of His attributes will inevitably comfort us, disturb us, or thrill us. Doxology is the inevitable outcome of a genuine encounter with God. Worship flows from our entire being.

Even though people are built differently in how they express their emotions, we all have something in common. Truth delivered in answer to a desperate need demands a response. Those who have been "redeemed of the Lord" must say so (Ps. 107:2). It is like the reaction to finding an oasis after traveling for miles in a vast and arid desert. No matter how stoic and reserved a person is, there must inevitably be an emotional reaction.

The truth is that we all know how to gaze intently at something. We do it every day. We gaze intently on our idols, for this is what it means to worship them. When we gaze on the beauty of something, we turn it over in our imagination. We meditate on it with intensity, examining all sides of it. We do this with whatever we imagine that we want. This could be anything or anyone. We fill our minds with it, mentally tasting it, resting in it, fantasizing about it, and becoming absorbed in it. Humans are built with this capacity for worship. The problem comes when we gaze at anything or anyone but God.

Spiritual integrity is wrapped up in receiving the grace to focus on the only real object of our devotion. Without this grace, our worship will inevitably be given to other objects. So we should pray for that grace, like the psalmist, "Turn away mine eyes from beholding vanity; and quicken thou me in thy way" (Ps. 119:37). Let us pray for the grace to gaze constantly at the right person.

Teach Me Your Way

The central phrase in verses 11–14 of Psalm 27 are the words, "Teach me thy way, O LORD." These words explain the verb *inquire* in verse 4. David is going beyond beholding or gazing upon the Lord. He is actively seeking the Lord, in order to integrate the Lord's agenda into his life. The order of our actions is important here, for if we seek to obey God without beholding the beauty of the Lord, we will likely become legalistic Pharisees. Our obedience is only meaningful if it is birthed in worship, and it will only be sustainable if it is rooted and grounded in doxology. This is true of all our relationships, not just our relationship with God. In marriage, our activities for our spouse are sterile and meaningless if they are not driven by internal intimacy, by gazing upon our spouse's beauty. Yet, on the other hand, our beholding must turn into inquiring; seeing the Lord's beauty must lead us to action.

A perfect example of how this works is recounted in the story of blind Bartimaeus (Mark 10:46–52). He knew our Lord Jesus would travel on a particular road, so he seated himself there (*dwelling*). Bartimaeus had not only heard that the Lord was coming that way, but he had also heard of what the Lord could do for him (*beholding*). Then, despite significant efforts by the crowd to quiet him down, he cried out more and more at his moment of opportunity: "Jesus, thou son of David, have mercy on me!" (v. 47; *inquiring*). Instead of engaging in a never-ending quest for secrets to success or hidden keys to victory, we need to seat ourselves on the road that we know that the Lord Jesus inevitably will come down, and ask Him to direct our steps.

If we wish to inquire into God's will, we must embrace the ordinary means of grace. We must meditate on God's inspired Word. We must pray without ceasing. We must regularly assemble with God's people in covenant worship. We must submit to the spiritual leadership of our pastors. We must conscientiously participate in the sacraments of baptism and the Lord's Supper. Additionally, we should pursue a simple lifestyle instead of materialism, chastity instead of impurity, and forgiveness instead of bitterness. It is written, "Hath the LORD as great delight in burnt offerings and sacrifices, as in obeying the voice of the LORD? Behold, to obey is better than sacrifice, and to hearken than the fat of rams" (1 Sam. 15:22). We must choose obedience instead of opportunism, initiative instead of idleness, exertion instead of equivocation, and pursuing God's agenda over the idolatrous interests of our hearts.

We may conclude our study of Psalm 27 where we began—in the temple. All this *dwelling, beholding,* and *inquiring* was to be done in the house of the Lord, in the temple. To understand the significance of this, we must look beyond the physical temple of ancient Israel. In John 2:19, Jesus said, "Destroy this temple, and in three days I will raise it up." When the religious leaders heard this, they were dumbfounded, thinking, "You are crazy! It took 40 years to build this temple. How in the world will you build it up in three days?" Yet John tells us that our Lord was referring to Himself (John 2:21). Jesus is the true temple, the reality which the physical temple could only foreshadow.

We need to emulate the path that David took. David watched the temple ritual and saw God's beauty through it. He saw animals constantly being slaughtered and offered up to God as sacrifices. In that, he saw the beauty of God's justice and holiness. He saw a God who requires that sin be paid for, a God who cannot overlook evil (Ex. 34:7). The God of the Bible is a good judge, and good judges must judge with integrity, taking into account the law and the facts of the case.

But David looked again at the sacrificial offerings, and he saw something else. He saw a merciful God who gave the Lamb of God who takes away the world's sin (John 1:29). He saw a God who found a way to forgive sins without compromising His justice. He found a God who pronounced the sentence of infinite punishment for an infinite debt of sin; yet at the same time, a God who surrendered His only begotten Son to suffer that ultimate penalty to cover our infinite debt.

This God whom David saw in the temple is our God whom we meet in the person of Jesus Christ. David saw the beauty and glory of the Lord, but so did the apostle Paul, who wrote "But we all, with open face beholding as in a glass the glory of the Lord, are changed into the same image from glory to glory, even as by the Spirit of the Lord" (2 Cor. 3:18). Here is the answer to the flood of negative events that confront us on every side. It is not seeking to run away from these negative thoughts or to turn our eyes from them. Rather, we must turn our eyes toward Jesus. He is the Way, the Truth, and the Life (John 14:6). Because of Him, all God's elect can say confidently with David, "I had fainted, unless I had believed to see the goodness of the LORD in the land of the living" (Ps. 27:13).

True disciples of Christ are not objective concerning this Jesus. Because of His grace, we are now totally biased; we have tasted and have seen that the Lord is good (Ps. 34:8). We thank God for both the smiling and frowning providences in our lives because we have found what we are looking for in Jesus. In the midst of the reversals and the rejections of life—the disappointments and the demotions, the stress and the strain, the problems and the pain, the shame and the stumbling, the rhetoric and the rambling, the pandemonium and the pandemics—we know that it is all for our good (Rom. 8:28). In Jesus, we have found what we are looking for and have been found by Him.

CONCLUSION

Making a call for a radical change must be justified. We have a natural aversion to anything radical: we generally need to be convinced that we are under attack, or facing some grave danger, to obey such a call. Hopefully, the case has been made in this short volume. We must ask ourselves a few questions as we ponder these issues going forward. How loyal are we to the cause of Christ and His church? Do we jealously guard and protect the legacy of faith once delivered to the saints?

Perhaps one of the most repugnant words in any language is its word for *traitor*. Few people are more despicable than those who betray their family, friends, cause, or nation. There are many examples of traitors in the Bible and history, but the name of the ultimate betrayer, Judas Iscariot, has become synonymous with the term *traitor*. In contrast, among the most treasured words in any language are *loyalty* and its synonyms: faithfulness, allegiance, fidelity, and devotion.

The Bible emphasizes the importance of loyalty. "Most men will proclaim every one his own goodness," Solomon wrote, "but a faithful man who can find?" (Prov. 20:6). Not all those who proclaim loyalty demonstrate it, but "he that followeth after righteousness and mercy findeth life, righteousness, and honour" (Prov. 21:21). Those in authority, Solomon added, must also display loyalty: "Mercy and truth preserve the king: and his throne is upholden by mercy" (Prov. 20:28). But of far greater significance than loyalty to any human person or cause is loyalty to God, which may be defined as loving Him with all one's heart, soul, mind, and strength (Mark 12:30; cf. Deut. 6:5).

Such loyalty does not come cheaply or easily. In Matthew 10:34–38, our Lord Jesus described the price allegiance to Him might exact. He said, "Think not that I am come to send peace on earth: I came not to send peace, but a sword. For I am come to set a man at variance against his father, and the daughter against her mother, and the daughter in law against her mother in law. And a man's foes shall be they of his own household. He that loveth father or mother more than me is not worthy of me: and he that loveth son or daughter more than me is not worthy of me. And he that taketh not his cross, and followeth after me, is not worthy of me." Loyalty to Jesus can be a sword that severs family ties or even costs people their lives—a truth attested to by the countless thousands of martyrs who preferred death to disloyalty.

The church has often proven unfaithful to the Lord. The apostle Paul confronted the apostle Peter's disloyalty (Gal. 2:11–13). He also rebuked the Galatians for their betrayal of the gospel of grace (Gal. 3:3). The apostle Peter and Jude warned of deceptive false teachers who would lead many astray from the truth (2 Peter 2:1–3, 10–22; Jude 4–16). James warned those who are not entirely loyal to God not to expect anything from Him (James 1:5–8). Indeed, five of the seven churches to whom the apostle John addressed the book of Revelation were disloyal to the Lord Jesus Christ (Rev. 2–3).

None of the New Testament writers were more concerned about loyalty than the apostle Paul, and nowhere was he more concerned about disloyalty than at Corinth. Deceived by the seductive lies of some self-appointed false apostles, many of the Corinthians had openly rebelled against Paul. The apostle dealt with that mutiny in a sternly worded letter (2 Cor. 2:1–4). As a result, most of the Corinthians repented and reaffirmed their loyalty to him (7:6–11). The apostle Paul knew, however, that the rebellion had not been completely put down but merely driven underground. Therefore, he addressed the repentant majority in the Corinthian assembly in 2 Corinthians 1–9, urging their continued loyalty to him. Then in chapters 10–13, he dealt firmly and directly with the false apostles and their unrepentant followers, defending himself against their vicious attacks on his character and ministry.

The apostle Paul found defending himself distasteful, and he abhorred self-commendation. Yet he could not permit the false teachers to destroy his reputation and undermine his teaching. They had exalted and promoted themselves (2 Cor. 10:12), and the Corinthians were impressed. If the apostle Paul did not defend himself, they would be cut off from him as the source of the divine truth and be at the mercy of the false teachers. His defense was not for his sake but theirs. As distasteful as it was to him, Paul had to defend his integrity—not for pride, self-exaltation, or his ego, but because the gospel was at stake.

Beginning in chapter 11, the apostle Paul confronted the false apostles. Reluctantly, he compared himself to them so the Corinthians could distinguish a faithful messenger of God from the false ones. As he began to confront the false apostles, Paul revealed that his motive for doing so was to call the Corinthians back to loyalty. He started by expressing his wish that they bear with him in his self-defense, which the apostle referred to as a bit of foolishness as he was about to answer the Corinthian fools as their folly deserved (Prov. 26:5). He softened the blow by acknowledging that they were indeed bearing with him—an affirmation of their positive response to his prior correction. He asked for the same favorable response as he defended himself against the false teachers' attacks and the Corinthians' foolish disloyalty.

In 2 Corinthians 11:2–6, the apostle Paul issued a four-count indictment of the Corinthians' disloyalty. The four issues are critical in evaluating our own loyalty to Christ and His church. We must protect the congregation of God's people. We must protect our covenant. We must protect our Christology. Finally, we must protect our communication.

Protecting Our Congregation

The thought of the Corinthian brethren being seduced into error by the false apostles was heartbreaking to the apostle Paul, so he said,

"I am jealous over you with godly jealousy" (2 Cor. 11:2). What may have seemed to the Corinthians to be boasting on his part was prompted by godly jealousy (literally, "the jealousy of God"). The apostle's jealousy on God's behalf manifested itself in righteous indignation at the possibility of the Corinthians' defection.

The apostle Paul longed for the Corinthians to remain loyal to him, not for his own sake, but because loyalty to him meant loyalty to Christ. God's jealousy for His holy name and His people is a prominent Old Testament theme. In Exodus 20:5, God said, "I the LORD thy God am a jealous God." Exodus 34:14 reveals that one of God's names is "Jealous." In Deuteronomy 4:24, the Lord is described as "a consuming fire, even a jealous God." Deuteronomy 32:16 and 21 reveal that the Lord's holy jealousy is provoked when His people worship idols. In Ezekiel 39:25, God declares, "I will be jealous for my holy name."

Like David, who wrote in Psalm 69:9, "For the zeal of thine house hath eaten me up; and the reproaches of them that reproached thee are fallen upon me," the apostle Paul felt pain when God was dishonored (2 Cor. 11:28). He was particularly concerned about those believers who were weak and led into sin (11:29). There may be some who are glad to see others fall, but the faithful saints of God feel the pain of the failures of others.

It should hurt us when our brethren in the church are hurting, when fellow believers lose their way and are disgraced. We should be burdened when those young in the faith make bad choices and have to live with the consequences. We should mourn when others victimize an offender who has wronged us in the same way. When the church's peace is threatened and the leaders are stressed, we should be driven to our knees. Concern for the spiritual safety of our congregation should motivate us to radical action.

Protecting Our Covenant

In 2 Corinthians 11:2–3, the apostle Paul expressed his concern over the Corinthians' disloyalty to the covenant made with Christ by using the analogy of betrothal and marriage. As is the case today, the main elements of a Jewish wedding were the betrothal (engagement) and the actual wedding ceremony. The betrothal period usually lasted about a year (though sometimes couples were betrothed as young children). The betrothed couple, though not allowed to consummate the union physically, were legally regarded as husband and wife; the betrothal could be broken only by death or divorce, and unfaithfulness during that time was considered adultery (see Matt. 1:18–19). The betrothal period culminated in the wedding ceremony, marking the completion of the covenant. During the betrothal period, the father of the bride was responsible for ensuring that his daughter remained faithful to her pledged husband. He would present her as a pure virgin at the wedding ceremony.

When the apostle Paul preached the gospel to the Corinthians, he betrothed them, as it were, to one husband—the Lord Jesus Christ. At salvation, they pledged their loyalty to Christ, and the apostle wanted to ensure that they remained faithful. As their spiritual father (1 Cor. 4:15), the apostle was determined to present them as pure virgins to Christ. Having been engaged to Him at salvation, the Corinthian church will be given to Christ at His return when Christ, as the Bridegroom, will come for the church, His bride.

The phrase, "But I fear," (2 Cor. 11:3) expresses the heart of the apostle Paul's concern, both in this passage and in the entire epistle. His defense of his integrity and his ministry, his appeals for the Corinthians' loyalty, and his confrontation with the false teachers were all motivated by a godly concern for their welfare. The apostle recognized the possibility that the false apostles could lead the Corinthians astray, and he warned them against this. He feared that some professing Christians in the church at Corinth would in the end prove not to have exercised saving faith in Christ—a concern that was magnified because the Corinthians demonstrated an alarming susceptibility to being seduced, welcoming those who preached another Jesus and a different gospel (11:4).

Every pastor fears that some of his sheep might go astray. As noted above, the apostle Paul's zeal for the purity of the churches caused him daily concern (2 Cor. 11:28). A heartbreaking theme throughout history is the disloyalty of many who claimed to be followers of Jesus Christ. Countless churches that name the name of Christ have been seduced by "seducing spirits" teaching "doctrines of devils" (1 Tim. 4:1) and become disloyal to Him.

The apostle Paul feared that Satan's emissaries, using the same craftiness by which their evil master deceived Eve (Gen. 3:1–5), would lead the Corinthians' minds astray, thus corrupting them (2 Cor. 11:13–15). The church's lack of discernment in these things is a significant problem because the spiritual battle is ideological (Eph. 4:14). The church's willingness to tolerate error in the name of unity, coupled with a lack of biblical and doctrinal knowledge, has crippled its ability to discern truth from error. As a result, it is too often easy prey for the ravenous wolves of whom both our Lord Jesus and the apostle Paul warned (Matt. 7:15; Acts 20:29). These wolves are determined to wound the church and sap its power. As radicals for Christ, we need to cultivate the ability to see through Satan's lies and combat them with God's truth.

The essence of the Christian life is simplicity and purity of devotion to Christ. To the Philippians, the apostle Paul wrote, "For to me to live is Christ, and to die is gain" (Phil. 1:21). Not to love Christ supremely as Savior and Lord is an act of disloyalty. False teachers shift the focus away from Jesus Christ and onto rituals, ceremonies, good works, miracles, emotional experiences, psychology, entertainment, political and social causes, and anything else that will distract people. Loyalty to the Lord Jesus Christ is nonnegotiable in the Christian life—so much so that the Scripture declares, "If any man love not the Lord Jesus Christ, let him be Anathema Maranatha" (1 Cor. 16:22).[1] Beloved, our faith is not that complicated. Let us trust Christ's work on our behalf alone, leaning on His active and passive obedience, His perfect life and atoning death. Let us fear God and keep His commandments. Let us do what God says and leave the rest to Him.

---

1. *Anathema*: cursed. *Maranatha*: Come, Lord!

Protecting Our Christology

False teachers had come to Corinth. Though God had not sent them, the Corinthians had welcomed them and given them a platform from which to proclaim their false gospel. These false apostles opposed the true knowledge of God and so distorted the truth that their so-called Jesus, Spirit, and gospel differed radically from what the apostle Paul preached. The different gospel of the opponents conformed to worldly ways of thinking to such a degree that the apostle and his apostolic ministry—a ministry manifesting the death of Jesus through adversity and suffering—were despised and rejected in favor of ministries that better fit cultural tastes of the time (such as eloquence, philosophical wisdom, and spectacular displays of spiritual power).

The apostle did not dignify the false teachers' heresy by giving a detailed explanation of it. But here, he summarized it under three general headings.

First, the false apostles preached another Jesus, not the true Lord Jesus Christ whom he preached. An aberrant Christology has always been a hallmark of false religions and cults. Instead of viewing Him as the eternal second person of the Trinity, who became a man and died as an atoning sacrifice for sin, they present Him as a prophet, a guru, a social or political revolutionary, Michael the archangel, a spirit child of God, an emanation from God—anything but the true God in the flesh. Although the false apostles outwardly identified with Jesus, the Jesus they preached was not the Jesus of Scripture.

Second, the false apostles came in the power of a different spirit, a demonic spirit, not the Holy Spirit whom the Corinthians had received at salvation. All false teaching ultimately derives from Satan and his demon hosts, whom the apostle Paul described as "seducing spirits" (1 Tim. 4:1), and the apostle John called "the spirit of error" (1 John 4:6).

Third, the false apostles preached a different gospel from the gospel that the Corinthians had accepted when the apostle Paul first preached it to them. This false gospel undoubtedly denied that salvation is by grace alone, through faith alone, in Christ alone, according to the Holy Scriptures alone, to the glory of God alone. Such a message must inevitably have added human works to God's grace. Yet the Corinthians listened to it patiently instead of rejecting this damnable heresy. They tolerated it, justifying the apostle Paul's fear for their purity.

Our Christology, our position on the nature of Jesus Christ, is the crux of our faith. If the Lord Jesus is not who He said He is, then we are not who we think we are. If He is not the spotless Lamb who shed His infinitely worthy blood, then we are still faced with our filthy record of sin and the fearsome prospect of an infinite hell. Christ Jesus is either man's only hope or this world is hopelessly and desperately out of options. He must be very God or we will never please God, for God will never be satisfied with the best work of corrupt sinners like us—only with the perfect offering of His own Son.

Protecting Our Communication

Despite the apostle Paul's hesitancy to boast, he asserted that he was not in the least inferior to the most eminent of the Corinthians' "apostles." He was not acknowledging them as his equals, since they were false apostles and he was a true apostle (cf. 2 Cor. 4:7–15; 6:4–10; 11:12–15, 21–33; 12:12). But for the sake of argument, he called on the Corinthians to at least grant that he was no lower than the "super-apostles," as they apparently styled themselves.

The false apostles scorned the apostle Paul for being "rude in speech" (2 Cor. 11:6). The word *rude* has a contemptuous ring to it, reflecting the false apostles' view that Paul was a crude, amateurish, and unrefined speaker. Paul acknowledged that he was not interested in the rhetorical and oratorical skills that impressed the Greeks because he was not concerned with technique but with the truth. His message was the gospel, clearly and straightforwardly presented, not a theatrical presentation designed to deceive his audience. He knew that human eloquence might draw people to the preacher, but it would not lead them to the cross. Faithful preaching, on the other hand, results not in people admiring the preacher, but rather in people adoring the subject of the proclamation—Christ. The gospel is "the power of God unto salvation" (Rom. 1:16) and does not need human embellishment.

The apostle Paul lays out his preaching philosophy in 1 Corinthians 1:17–25:

> For Christ sent me not to baptize, but to preach the gospel: not with wisdom of words, lest the cross of Christ should be made of none effect. For the preaching of the cross is to them that perish foolishness; but unto us which are saved it is the power of God. For it is written, I will destroy the wisdom of the wise, and will bring to nothing the understanding of the prudent. Where is the wise? where is the scribe? where is the disputer of this world? hath not God made foolish the wisdom of this world? For after that in the wisdom of God the world by wisdom knew not God, it pleased God by the foolishness of preaching to save them that believe. For the Jews require a sign, and the Greeks seek after wisdom: but we preach Christ crucified, unto the Jews a stumblingblock, and unto the Greeks foolishness; but unto them which are called, both Jews and Greeks, Christ the power of God, and the wisdom of God. Because the foolishness of God is wiser than men; and the weakness of God is stronger than men (cf. 1 Cor. 2:1–5).

It is not that the apostle Paul was an ineffective speaker. On the contrary, he spoke with tremendous power and impact. But he was not interested in flowery oratory or merely persuasive words of human wisdom. His goal was to preach the gospel of Christ lucidly and with conviction, using all his mind and heart, so that the faith of his hearers would not rest on the wisdom of men but the power of God.

Although his communication skills might have been deficient by the false apostles' standards, the apostle Paul was certainly not lacking in knowledge (2 Cor. 11:6). The false apostles claimed to have secret knowledge that was not available to the uninitiated. But the apostle Paul was a steward of the mysteries of God (1 Cor. 4:1), with profound insight into the mystery of Christ (Eph. 3:4). Nor did the apostle Paul keep his knowledge secret, but rather, by every possible means, he made the truth plain to the Corinthians. He had said the same thing to the church at Ephesus, testifying, "For I have not shunned to declare unto you all the counsel of God" (Acts 20:27). He had proclaimed among them the true knowledge of God's mystery—that is, Christ Himself (Col. 2:2).

Despite their solid, apostolic doctrinal foundation, the Corinthians were in grave danger of being seduced, as are we today. The risk of wandering from the truth and becoming confused and disloyal is a constant threat to the church of Jesus Christ. The apostle forcefully rebuked the Galatian churches, expressing his amazement that they were "so soon removed from him that called you into the grace of Christ unto another gospel" (Gal. 1:6). Five of the seven churches that the apostle John addressed in Revelation 2–3—churches founded under the apostle Paul's influence—were in danger of defecting from the gospel. That tragic pattern has been repeated throughout the church's history. Therefore, absolute loyalty to God's church, our covenant, our Christology, and our communication of the gospel are nonnegotiable principles for everyone who names the name of Christ.

We live in an age that shuns controversy and extreme positions, but if there is anything in our lives that is worth fighting for it is these things. We cannot sit by and watch these things being degraded or diluted. True believers in Christ must be radical in their orientation because they have something of the highest value to protect. Our objectives are no longer temporal but eternal—our passion is to please God, not our fleshly appetites. We have learned that satisfaction is only to be found in authentic intimacy with Christ. So let us guard the treasure we have found in Christ alone with everything that we have and everything that we are! He alone is worthy of such commitment of heart, mind, soul, and body.